PRAISE FOR *UNBINDING THE HEART*

"Agapi Stassinopoulos is an authentic, genuine, and inspirational writer and speaker who knows how to connect with and move her audience. She brings out the beauty, power, and independence in all of us."

— **Deepak Chopra**, author of *War of the Worldviews*

*"Besides being a loving sister, Agapi has an innate wisdom and a gift for communicating it to her readers. The insight and passion that she brings to **Unbinding the Heart**, and the lessons it holds for bringing freedom and grace into our lives, make it a must-read book."*

— **Arianna Huffington**, president and editor-in-chief of The Huffington Post Media Group

"I laughed, I cried, I got a craving for hummus . . . read this book, it's smashing."

— **Tracey Ullman**

"A joyous, loving, generous romp!"

— **Seth Godin**, author of *Poke the Box*

"Agapi shares her heart with us through her personal stories, full of hope and possibilities, and inspires us to open our own hearts to more loving for ourselves and others."

— **Donna Karan**, founder of Urban Zen

*"**Unbinding the Heart** is like a sumptuous Greek feast. It is a place filled with family, friends, and lovers, offering sustenance for the mind and spirit. Agapi's colorful stories are full of spiritual depth and personal insight, which will nourish the soul of her readers."*

— **Lisa Oz**, author of *Us*

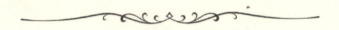

UNBINDING
THE
HEART

UNBINDING
THE
HEART

A DOSE OF GREEK WISDOM, GENEROSITY, AND UNCONDITIONAL LOVE

AGAPI STASSINOPOULOS

HAY HOUSE, INC.
Carlsbad, California • New York City
London • Sydney • Johannesburg
Vancouver • Hong Kong • New Delhi

Published and distributed in the United States by: Hay House, Inc.: www.hayhouse.com • **Published and distributed in Australia by:** Hay House Australia Pty. Ltd.: www.hayhouse.com.au • **Published and distributed in the United Kingdom by:** Hay House UK, Ltd.: www.hayhouse.co.uk • **Published and distributed in the Republic of South Africa by:** Hay House SA (Pty), Ltd.: www.hayhouse .co.za • **Distributed in Canada by:** Raincoast: www.raincoast .com • **Published in India by:** Hay House Publishers India: www .hayhouse.co.in

Cover design: Julie Davison • *Interior design:* Jenny Richards

Library of Congress Cataloging-in-Publication Data

Stassinopoulos, Agapi
  Unbinding the heart : a dose of Greek wisdom, generosity, and unconditional love / Agapi Stassinopoulos. — 1st ed.
     p. cm.
   ISBN 978-1-4019-3073-8 (hbk. : alk. paper) 1. Stassinopoulos, Agapi. 2. Self-realization. 3. Conduct of life. I. Title.
   BJ1470.S73 2012
   170'.44—dc23
                                                    2011034868

4761 7005 7/12

Hardcover ISBN: 978-1-4019-3073-8
Digital ISBN: 978-1-4019-3075-2

15 14 13 12   4 3 2 1
1st edition, February 2012

Printed in the United States of America

To Christina and Isabella,
whom I love with all my heart.

ALL, EVERYTHING THAT I UNDERSTAND,
I UNDERSTAND ONLY BECAUSE I LOVE.

—FROM *WAR AND PEACE* BY LEO TOLSTOY

CONTENTS

PREFACE

As I write this, I am sitting in our garden in the shade of the lemon tree we planted in honor of my mother when she passed, to celebrate her life, which was all about bearing fruit. Sitting here, I feel a profound gratitude for the values she instilled in me and the inner resources she gave me that have shaped the way I live my life now. By giving me my name—Agapi, which in Greek means "unconditional love"—she was laying the tracks that were mine to follow, the path of living with a loving, open heart. Her presence is palpable as I share my story with you. I write it out of a deep desire to share how I came to know the truth of my own heart and realize the fullness and freedom that were available beyond the barriers I placed around it.

I was brought up in Athens, in a culture where an open heart is celebrated and exuberance is encouraged. We eat, dance, make love, nap, tell people how we really feel, argue, make up, give, and then give some more. We open our homes to friends and strangers, share what we have, and bond very deeply with the people we love. Life is to be lived to the fullest. I was raised by a mother filled with the spirit of courage and generosity and an unshakable trust in life—a spirit that, in the face of adversity, soared even higher. And I had a father whose motto was "Ride life like a horse—grab it by the mane and hang on."

My mother and father's relationship was both passionate and turbulent, with a current of love that ran very deep but couldn't carry them through daily life. My parents' lives, so intricately intertwined with mine, would ultimately help me understand what causes our hearts to close and how we can learn to open them again. And they would teach me that love doesn't come with a fairy-tale ending of happily ever after.

I grew up thinking I would become a dancer. In the free, nonlinear expression of the art form, I found an outlet for all the things I felt but couldn't say. There on the stage, I would find a place to express my heart's tenderness, to go beyond the hurt and find my joy. When I was 14, I was chosen to dance the part of the narrator in a recital on the theme of "The Cosmos"; the other students were the planets, and my role was to tell their stories. That performance was the first time I felt the magic of captivating an audience. As the storyteller, I found that I could connect with them in a place where time was suspended, and for a moment, it was as if all of us were one.

Storytelling, of course, was part of my Greek heritage. The Greeks—the ultimate storytellers—created their myths out of thin air. They saw the elements and primal forces at work in the world, and the emotions within us, and they made gods of them all. For centuries, the Greeks told those stories to make sense of the world. And after my first experience as a storyteller, I was hooked. My dance teacher even encouraged me to pursue acting.

A few years later I went to London to study drama. There, I seemed to unleash a talent for the art that was rooted in my very cells. However, my natural Greek openness had to make some adjustments to adapt in a culture where people contained themselves for politeness' sake, and I channeled my expression into acting. On the stage, as I delved deep into the hearts of the characters I played, my own emotional life seemed to flourish. I was finding my bearings, and the acknowledgment I received from my teachers and directors was extremely gratifying. Soon after, I was asked to come to America to make a movie, and I thought I was on my way to becoming a star. Little did I know that my adventure in America would lead not to stardom, but to a soul journey in which I would peel away the layers and come to know my *self*.

Little by little, I would lay a foundation on which I could build my own character and find expression in ways more true to who I was. I would discover the tremendous value in being open with myself, with others, and with life, as all sorts of new opportunities—for creativity, work, growth, relationships—began to appear. I would learn the joy of letting my love out with no expectation of the outcome, but simply because that was the most liberating course of action. The irony was that most of my transformation came when things didn't work out and I didn't get what I thought I wanted. I found out that there are no happy endings, because there are no endings, but continuous, endless beginnings—opportunities to go deeper into ourselves to discover the miraculous truth of who we are.

There are no seven or eight simple steps to unbind our hearts, but there is one choice that we all have, and this is our golden opportunity in every moment of every day, whatever small or big challenges it brings: *Do I shut down or do I choose to open up one more time, even deeper?* In this book, I share with you some of the experiences that led me to that knowledge. I'm sharing my stories with you in the greatest hope that I can help a few other hearts loosen the knots that bind them.

When I awakened to that knowledge, my work found me. One of the ways it came was in the form of stories—the stories of the Greek goddesses. As if a dam had burst, I poured my creativity into writing, performing, and teaching about the goddesses and the archetypes they embody. I took them all over the world, and that is when I experienced the real power of stories to help us all awaken. But most of all, I experienced people's hearts. I saw how everyone, every single person, has a story that holds the truth of their heart, and those stories need to be heard. We need to tell our stories, as much as we need to listen to others'. And that is how our hearts unbind—with the simple message *You matter. My heart hears yours.*

How would your life be if you lived with a heart fully open and free and you knew that your story mattered? Think about this for a moment as you come and sit down with me. Imagine we're sitting under an olive tree on a midsummer afternoon, sharing a Greek picnic of olives, feta cheese, fresh garden tomatoes, home-baked bread, a wonderful chilled Greek wine, some watermelon and some grapes, and sharing the joy of simply being alive. While the breeze wafts away our worries, I offer you my stories, from my open heart to yours.

CHAPTER 1

THE TAPESTRY OF LIFE

When I was a little girl, I used to ask my mother to tell me my favorite story. It wasn't a fairy tale, it wasn't the Greek myths, it wasn't Aesop's fables or Hans Christian Andersen. It was the story of how she and my father met.

The Second World War had ended, and my mother, Elli, was recovering in her hometown of Thessaloniki in northern Greece after serving tirelessly in the Red Cross. One of her best friends, who would later marry one of her five brothers, invited her to go along on a visit to the countryside around Athens so she could rest, recover, and reclaim some of the fun of life. One lovely summer evening, they and a few other girlfriends decided to take a walk to their favorite hotel café and treat themselves to ice cream, the Greek specialty *kaimaki,* flavored with orchid root. They were walking through lush streets where the smell of jasmine hung in the air, past houses draped with pale purple wisteria, chatting and laughing, regaining their freedom after the war and the German occupation, when they got lost. They ran into a group of men who were lounging on the low wall along the sidewalk, smoking and basking in the air of a relaxed summer evening. One of the girls asked them if they knew how to get to the hotel. In a very traditional Greek male way, the men replied, "We'll take you there." So they all walked together to the hotel. One of those men was my father, Costas.

Ice cream was served—big scoops of kaimaki, thick and creamy—drinks were poured, and vital connections started to happen. He and my mother started talking, and they talked for hours. My father told her that he had published an underground newspaper in support of the resistance during the occupation. One night the Germans had come to his house, pounded on the door, and arrested him. He was taken away to the concentration camp outside Athens, and later to Germany, where he was held for a year and a half before the war came to an end. He told my mother how he'd survived by working on a book that he had been writing, about his vision of modern Greece. Not on paper—he wouldn't have been allowed that—but in his head. At night, on his narrow bed, he edited that book line by line, and it kept his mind and soul alive.

My mother told him about caring for the wounded near the front lines and in a makeshift hospital high in the mountains, and about hiding Jewish families in her own family's home, at the risk of all their lives. Each of them was a hero in the other's eyes. By the end of the evening they had fallen for each other completely, and their epic love story had begun. When my father went back to his house that night, he told his mother, "I have met an angel." It was a great moment—destiny, fate, and the stars aligned.

I was raised in Greece with olive oil, feta cheese, and the principle of synchronicity as fare. I had a mother who lived it, breathed it, and affirmed it daily. And my own life was synchronicity in action, from the very start.

Five years after that night at the Athens café, my parents married and had a daughter—my sister, Arianna. Though their love was passionate, their life together was anything but settled. My father stayed out late at nightclubs with his friends, shut my mother out, then exploded when she criticized him. Whenever she asked him, "Where have you been?" he would retort, "I forbid you to interfere with my private life." When she got pregnant again a few years later, they didn't want another child, so they decided that she would have an abortion, and she made the appointment with the doctor. The day the abortion was scheduled, she woke early and was getting out of bed when my father reached for her. Their intimate moment in bed that morning made my mother miss her appointment, and she never made another one. She ended up having the baby—me. Synchronicity working in my favor!

I was brought up with the notion that connections happen, threads come together, and in this way, life moves you forward, weaving you into a tapestry of its own design. When I was 12 years old, my mother introduced me to yoga. Years later, yoga would lead me through the doorway to my true self.

When I was 14, I noticed one of my classmates carving letters into the wood of her desk: R-A-D-A. I asked her what it meant. "It's the Royal Academy of Dramatic Art in London," she said. "I want to go there." As soon as she said it, I knew I wanted to study there too. I told my mother, who said, as if she knew it for a fact, "That's where you're going." And in the years that followed, a series of stepping-stones—chance meetings, perfect timings—fell into place to take me just where I wanted to go.

When I was 16, my mother gave me a book of Carl Jung's writings on the archetypes, universal patterns of behavior and emotion within the human psyche. It was an English version, and although my English wasn't up to the standard of such intellectual material, I kept reading anyway, out of fascination. Fifteen years later, when my sister was commissioned to write a book on the gods of Greece, I ended up helping her with the research, and I started to understand the power of the gods, which are, after all, archetypes in action. The seed my mother had planted was sprouting.

Fast-forward a decade from my work with my sister on the gods: I've written and performed a one-woman show in New York called *Conversations with the Goddesses*—the stories of the Greek goddesses applied to us today—and the right person is in the audience at the right time to help me take the next step. Soon my show is on videotape and finds its way into the hands of a wonderful visionary publisher. She commissions *me* to write my first book, based on the stories in the show. Those powerful archetypes become my life's work for the next ten years, until I have integrated them so fully that that piece is complete and I can move into the next phase of my work—the book you're reading now.

Frame after frame, the images of my life form a thread of synchronicity. It has given me greater trust and confidence in dealing with the people around me; it's taught me not to panic when things don't seem to go my way, and to expect wondrous happenings on a daily basis. Synchronicity is in my DNA, as I feel it is in everyone's. I would say that relying on it has become second nature, but it's more accurate to say that it *is* our nature. It's the thread that holds our whole gorgeous tapestry together.

To me, synchronicity is the manifestation in the physical world of connections that are forming in the invisible world all the time. It is the energy that sustains the cosmos, moves the atoms, and breathes in our cells, making itself known to us so we remember that the Divine is always at work within us and for us. It is proof that we are made from more than the flesh and bones of our dense materiality—that we are part of a larger, unseen picture. The philosopher William James observed that we are like islands in the sea, separated on the surface but connected in the deep. We are all in the dance together. And when our hearts are open, when we allow love to move through us in this dance of life, love transforms our steps so that each one is perfect.

As I look back at my life, I am in awe of the perfection with which things unfold beyond our control despite all of our doubts. I know that we are all connected in the deep beneath the surface of things, just as my mother and my father were, before their two groups of friends came together on that Athens street. Though they didn't know each other yet, something larger knew them both, and life was moving them forward.

CHAPTER 2

ALWAYS A SOLUTION

It was six o'clock on a Saturday evening, and my mother and my sister and I were on our way out the door to see a George Bernard Shaw play at one of the most popular theaters in Athens. We were going to get a taxi to the theater in time for the seven o'clock curtain and then have dinner afterward. My sister and I were rushing around in excitement; we loved to go to plays with our mom. We rushed out the door toward the elevator. As the door swung shut behind us, a look of sudden realization crossed my mother's face. She had left her handbag inside the apartment.

"Open the door and we'll get it," we urged her.

"I can't," she said. "My keys are in my handbag!"

My sister and I were panicked—but my mother was perfectly calm. Never did it occur to her that we'd have to cancel our plans and call a locksmith. In the philo-sophical way she had, she said to us, "We just need to find another solution."

Down she went to the superintendent's apartment. She had done a lot for the super's family over the years, from helping the children get into good schools to help-ing them get a new washing machine; taking care of people in that way was the essence of life to her. So when she asked to borrow some money for the evening, her request was instantly granted. One obstacle overcome.

Once our taxi deposited us at the theater, our next obstacle to face was the fact that we didn't have our tick-ets: they were in her handbag too! I thought it was hope-less. The show was sold out, and we didn't have enough money to buy three new tickets anyway. But my mother could charm people so completely that it seemed al-most magical sometimes, and she had a gift for break-ing through the barriers people put up with their rules and regulations. In her disarming way, she explained to the box office manager what had happened. He said that if we waited until everyone else had gone in, he would try to seat us—and when they had, he gave us the three seats that remained empty.

My sister and I were still worried: how would we get back into the apartment when we got home? Whenever we asked my mother, though, she would say, "No wor-ries. Let's enjoy the play. We will find a way." So we en-joyed the play thoroughly, then went out for a lovely dinner and took another taxi back home. We still didn't know how we would get inside, but my mother had said we'd find a way.

It so happened that our apartment building was right across the street from the fire station. My mother went over and spoke to the fire chief to see if they could put one of their ladders up to the third floor. And they did! The chief himself went up the ladder, climbed in our window, and opened the door for us from the inside. The next day, to thank the firemen, my mother sent a large tray of cookies across the street.

It might seem strange for someone whose nature was so fundamentally giving to be put in a position where she was compelled to receive instead. In fact, though, my mother was showing my sister and me that true giving and receiving arise from the same free and generous source in us. She knew it was important to receive in a spirit of abundance rather than of need—to ask for help not with a sense of entitlement, but with simple trust that help was always there, waiting to be accessed. She used to say to me, "Don't go into the world wanting. Go thinking about what you can give. And you will get what you want, because you won't be going in as a beggar or a miser or starting from a position of lack." She taught us that the way to achieve the outcomes we wanted was to have absolutely no doubt in our hearts that it was going to be so, because we had declared it so.

My mother wasn't afraid to ask. Asking, for her, was not a sign of weakness or a source of the slightest discomfort. Because she wasn't bound by notions of how things should happen, she didn't second-guess herself: *Oh, I really shouldn't ask the super for money.* She didn't anticipate failure: *What if we can't get in without our tickets?* And, most of all, she didn't let it ruin her evening—she didn't allow those obstacles to take away any of her joy. She just stated what she needed with confidence and authenticity. And things had a way of working out, maybe for that very reason. We all know people who seem to have trouble admitting they need help or accepting it when it's offered to them. It's as if there's some sort of block. When you ask for help in my mother's spirit, you're removing that block, preparing a place within yourself where you can receive.

All her life my mother embraced the impossible, from opening a locked apartment door to getting her daughters into the best English schools to giving us a rich experience of life even when the rent was overdue. That was the epitome of my mother: in the midst of her adversity, she refused to worry about problems. She would sit there in her wise presence, as if she were tuning in to eternity, and simply command herself to come up with solutions. It was wondrous to watch.

"When you worry," she used to say, "you're moving yourself away from your center, and it's much harder to function effectively. When you stop worrying, you come back into balance." Thanks to her, I, too, see the world as a place of boundless abundance from which we can choose and create solutions to whatever problems we face. The world is filled with people who can come to our aid, and we are not alone, if we are willing to ask and open to receive.

CHAPTER 3

BEING
VALIDATED

When I was in school, I struggled terribly with math, and I felt so inadequate because I couldn't get it. I can't describe how utterly unintelligible algebra was to me. If you asked me to recite Shakespeare from memory, I'd do it with ease and joy, but quadratic equations eluded me completely. So I did what any adolescent girl would do: I prayed that my math teacher would die and we wouldn't have math class anymore. I prayed that school policy would change so that math would be imposed only as a cruel punishment for girls who did very bad things. And I prayed that the school would be banned altogether from teaching math to those of us (me, really) who had a mental math-block. In my mind, these were the only things that could make the world good again.

I hated feeling inadequate. I hated seeing how easily other girls got it and wondering what was wrong with me. But I was blessed to have a mother who validated me every time I turned around. She saw where my gifts lay, and she reinforced them. She kept saying to me, "Darling, you are not here to be good at math. You are good in the arts. That's your love—theater and dancing—and that's what you are going to do. Let's just pass that useless class."

One day after school, I was doing homework in my room when the doorbell rang. When I opened the apartment door, who should be standing there but Mrs. Michalopoulos, my math teacher. "Mrs. Michalopoulos," I said, a little embarrassed that I'd been wishing she would die, "what are you doing here?"

"I am here to give you private lessons," she said. "Didn't your mother tell you?"

She hadn't told me. She had simply come up with a plan to help me where I was stuck so that I could focus my energy where it would flourish. All I needed to do was pass the final exam—and Mrs. Michalopoulos would be the one giving the exam! So, in the course of the private lessons, without giving anything away, she was preparing me for the very problems I would be facing.

I did pass that class, and the next, and the next. At the end of each semester, my mother went to the school to get Arianna's and my grades, and each time she came home with flowers—anemones—for both of us, saying, "Congratulations! You passed!" When I asked her what grades I had received, she would say, "It doesn't matter. You passed—that's all that matters." She knew how to identify our essential gifts, and so she never compared us to each other. She would never say to me, "Look how good Arianna is at math. Why can't you be more like her?" She would never say to Arianna, "Look what a great dancer Agapi is. Why can't you dance like her?" Instead, she saw and supported our unique potential. In doing so, she was giving us both an extraordinary gift.

In the philosophy of Aristotle, there is a word for potential blossoming into being. He coined this term, *entelecheia—entelechy* in English—to describe both a process and a state of completeness: a possibility actualized, an essence fully realized, a conception finding its full-blown form. To put it another way, entelechy means things becoming what they are.

I think of entelechy when I look at my beautiful nieces—young adults at such an early stage on their journeys, with so much ahead of them and yet so much unknown. I see their potential, their unique gifts and possibilities, the essence of greatness in each of them. I see *who they are,* and I am holding the vision for them as they grow into their being. I like to think that God sees all of us this way.

Entelechy is the seed that sprouts to be the orchard. When we see our own gifts and greatness, we're helping ourselves to blossom, too. We are fertilizing the soil of our lives so that we, too, grow into who we know we can be. But we need to see past our perceived faults in order to honor our gifts.

When my mother brought us anemones after viewing our report cards, it was not a reward for our grades. It was a tribute offered in the spirit of love, acknowledging who we were. That's the truest validation we can ever have, and all of us at some point have to learn to do it for ourselves. The value of who we are, just as we are, can never be taken away from us, whether people praise us or criticize us, whether the world acknowledges us or not.

Recently I was leaving a hotel in Los Angeles and I needed to get my car. I took my parking receipt to the concierge and asked him if he wouldn't mind validating me. He looked me right in the eye and said, "Sure. You are beautiful."

I laughed! He laughed, too. And, as funny as it was, it also felt good.

To be validated is to be seen, and seen for who we are. Simply being told that we are loved is validation. Speaking our feelings and being heard is also sheer validation. And knowing that we matter is validation too. Feeling validated creates a foundation for us to flourish. The world will do what the world will do—but when we are feeling validated inside, it's remarkable how the world starts to reflect that back to us.

CHAPTER 4

"MUMMY, ARE WE RICH?"

My father had a passion for horse racing. Sunday mornings and Wednesday afternoons were his outlet for the excitement of betting and winning (but mostly losing). Every Sunday morning, one of his friends picked him up to go to the racetrack about an hour away. I would watch at the window for the shiny blue Jaguar to pull up in front of the house. His friend would wait in the backseat while the driver got out to hold the door. We lived in a lovely but modest house in the suburbs of Athens and used taxis or took the bus to go into the city. We didn't have a car, and my father had never learned to drive.

My father's friend with the Jaguar lived farther outside the city, in a mansion with a staff and the countless little luxuries that money brings. When we visited his house, we saw movies in a screening room and had three-course dinners at a long dining-room table overlooking the well-tended gardens. Our house was much smaller—in fact, it was smaller than the homes of most of the people we knew—and much simpler inside, with no butler and no screening room. But our home always had music and food and an abundance of joy. In its relaxed atmosphere, there was nothing buttoned up; expression reigned supreme. Inside our friend's home, there was a sense of oppression instead. I always felt a sadness and a heaviness when I went there.

As young as I was, though, I could see that my father attached a great deal of importance to those occasions. He himself had never accumulated much money, because his focus was on ideas and ideals; the newspapers he published were intellectual triumphs but not successful business ventures. I would often hear him say to my mother, "I have some important people coming for dinner tonight," or "We are going out with some very important people." Your thinking shifts when you hear a statement like that, especially when you are young. *Oh! Important people! I must behave in a certain way to accommodate these important people. I must alter myself, be someone I am not, so they will be impressed with me.* I had seen that my father himself spoke and acted a certain way when he was around them, different from the way he behaved around people he worked with or friends who didn't have fancy cars.

The sight of the shiny blue Jaguar in our driveway was a conditioned cue—*here is my father's rich friend coming to take him to the races*—that, week after week, triggered that same response in me. The hierarchy of life was clicking into place. *It's the other people who have more and we have less, so we must be less,* says the nine-year-old consciousness. *Those are the rich people, and I am not one of them.*

I knew that my mother was different from my father in some basic way, because she treated all people the same, and she herself behaved the same, no matter whom she was with. She had no status handicap, and it freed her. My father was much more attuned to hierarchy, and I saw how it hindered him, though he was a brilliant and exceptional man. One Sunday morning after he and his friend drove off, I burst out to my mother with the innocence of a puzzled nine-year-old. "Mummy," I asked her, "are we rich?"

In a matter-of-fact tone that I can still hear, confident in her knowledge, she said, "We are very, very wealthy." And then she gave me the Talk—not the sex talk but the wealth talk. "Being rich doesn't mean you are wealthy. Being rich means you have a lot of money. Being wealthy means you value the gifts you have and you develop them. Wealth means that you have everything you need, and that you share it, too. It means being generous with what you have, not living in fear of losing what you have, and not comparing it to what anyone else has." Her passion was palpable as she spoke about these ideas. "Having intelligence is wealth. Being curious about life is wealth. Ethics is wealth—it is the integrity you have in all your relationships. Having friends who care for you and love you, and whom you care for and love, that is wealth. Taking care of yourself and being healthy is wealth, and so is having respect for yourself and your fellow human beings. Being educated, having a thirst for learning, being able to go to good schools with inspiring teachers who will help you

17

cultivate your talents, is wealth too—the most important kind, because without that, it really doesn't matter
what else you have." She went on: "The arts and culture are wealth. The artists of the world are all wealthy.
They have gifts that money can never buy. And if you
know how wealthy you are, *then* you can go make money—but only if you want to." In her enthusiasm, she
started writing things down for me on a piece of paper.
She wrote the words *Values* and *Ethics* and *Responsibility*
and *Inquiring Mind*. I was nine, but that didn't stop her.
She was letting me know that I need never feel intimi-
dated or make myself less because other people had bigger bank accounts or cars or houses. She was infusing
me with her wisdom, raising me to stand tall in myself
and meet life with confidence and a generous spirit.
She knew that then I would feel no sense of lack, but be
enriched by all the people and experiences that came
my way.

She made sure of that, even when it wasn't clear where
the resources would come from. I was only 12 when she
separated from my father and suddenly had to make her
own way. Then her vision for her daughters, together
with her trust in life and her unabashed willingness to ask
for help, moved her forward to find solutions.

As the years went on, I saw my mother interact with
all kinds of people, many of whom were exorbitantly
rich and many of whom were not. Together we went to
the country house of Lord and Lady So-and-So, where
everything was served on silver platters, and to the one-
bedroom apartment of the struggling actor, where the
kitchen table and the bed were only a few feet apart. My
mother was not one bit more impressed by the silver
platters than by the apartment.

She moved in the most sophisticated circles—the English aristocracy, the intellectual and artistic elite of Athens and London, Los Angeles, and New York—surrounded by money and position, talent and fame. She spoke wonderful English, French, and German as well as Greek, which in itself gave her the ability to easily move between worlds. She was well-read, but she also had a deeper intelligence that went far beyond a familiarity with all the right books. She had the ability to lower people's defenses and engage them at the level that mattered to them most, no matter how elevated they were perceived to be. She never put them into categories like "rich" or "important," and she never compared herself to them; she carried herself with the confidence of her own authenticity. And nothing about other people truly impressed her except *their* authenticity. With her warmth and her inclusiveness, she broke down people's worldly facades.

For a time, while we lived in London, my sister was dating a politician, and we gave a dinner at our home for the prime minister. As the party was getting under way, it so happened that a plumber was arriving, too, to open a clogged drain in the kitchen. When the plumber heard that the prime minister was coming to dinner, he was clearly impressed. "I supported him last election," he said.

"Would you like to meet him?" my mother inquired. And while the guests were making themselves comfortable in the living room, she went and asked the prime minister if he wouldn't mind saying hello to one of his supporters. "Gladly," he replied, and he walked straight into the kitchen, where my mother introduced him to the plumber as if it were the most natural thing in the world, because to her it was.

She reached people with her personal stories, her strong opinions, her irreverent humor, her philosophy of life—and always with food! Everyone loves food, so feeding people was often the first step she took to connect. In a London taxi, the kind with the divider between passenger and driver, she would slide the glass to one side and ask the driver if he would like some nuts or an apple. Often the driver would be, understandably, taken aback: "I beg your pardon, madam?" To which she would simply say again: "Would you like an apple?" Some drivers refused, but sometimes one would accept. So, before she got out of the taxi, she reached across the barrier and put a piece of fruit in the driver's hand.

Later, when she and my sister and I moved to Los Angeles, we entertained a lot—elegant dinners for 20 or 30 people at a time, with catering services and waiters to feed the guests. Without fail, every party ended with my mother in the kitchen feeding the staff—talking to them, filling their plates, pouring them wine. It was inconceivable to her that the people who were serving us would not be taken care of and served in their turn.

Under my mother's guidance, I grew up having no sense of hierarchy in the world, just a feeling of our fundamental sameness. This is how my mother put it: if a group of people were on a sinking ship, it wouldn't matter who they were or what they did for a living. You wouldn't rescue the first-class passengers first and the cabin stewards last; you would reach out to them all. So why should it be any different when the ship isn't sinking?

Living by her example, surrounded by the warmth of her open mind and generous spirit, helped me develop a sense of myself that would not change whether people had more or less material success or worldly acclaim than I had. It was wonderful to be able to meet people without making these judgments—not evaluating them on the basis of what they had achieved or collected materially in order to decide how I should behave with them. I didn't need to alter *me* to fit some perception of what other people expected. It was so liberating to know I could simply, authentically, be myself—and enjoy and be enriched by the authentic gifts of others.

Other people could sense this freedom in me. And the more I shared of myself, the more I discovered that everyone, no matter what they had or didn't have, wanted connection. Essentially we all want to know that we matter—we want to be seen and valued for who we are. Ultimately, that is the greatest gift we can give each other. The greatest thing we can do for others is not so much to share our riches with them as to help them recognize their own inner wealth.

Little did I know that on that Sunday morning long ago, my mother was planting such a vital seed for my philosophy of life. Once I stopped worrying about how I would behave when the "important people" showed up, I could keep myself open to make real connections and meet people wherever I found them, as my mother did her whole life long. Those moments of connection are what make our lives full and truly rich. Although when my mother died, she had practically nothing in her bank account, she was the wealthiest woman I'd ever known.

CHAPTER 5

MEETING YOUR TEACHER

Theater was a part of my life from the very beginning. My sister's godmother was one of the most famous Greek tragediennes of her day, so going to the ancient theaters in Epidaurus and Athens was a big part of our social and cultural life. I grew up with Antigone, Elektra, Andromache, and Klytemnestra as my heroines and archetypes: women who expressed the depth and range of human passion, from rage to pain to anguish, ecstasy, and all-consuming love. As I watched those Greek plays I wondered how it would feel to be so free that you could openly express your larger-than-life feelings. And it seemed magical to be able to snap out of your own reality and become a completely different person—and on top of that, have an attentive audience!

The seed of acting had been planted. So, at 14, when I heard about the Royal Academy of Dramatic Art in London, something clicked. I wanted to go there and study even though knew very little about it. In my heart I knew it was where I was meant to be.

RADA had turned out the likes of Laurence Olivier, John Gielgud, Maggie Smith, Alan Rickman, and Kenneth Branagh. Never mind that they accepted 8 girls and 20 boys each year out of the thousand who auditioned, or that the rest of the people auditioning spoke the Queen's English as their first language. I had something they didn't have: I had my mother. She knew what it meant to have a vision, and she knew how to make it happen. She moved to England so that my sister could study economics at Cambridge, and when I finished high school, I joined my mother in London to take private acting lessons from a woman who taught at RADA.

At that age, I didn't yet have a strong sense of myself. *Who am I in the world?* I would ask. *What am I to become? Where will I fit in?* I was looking for the key that would unlock the door so that I would know, *Yes, this is mine to do; this is who I am.* We all have the seeds within us from a young age, but who is going to help us cultivate them? That's where our teachers come in—the gardeners of the bare soil that, if tended right, will bear fruit.

My teacher, Ada Mather, was American; she had taught acting at RADA for years, and she taught privately as well. The private classes were held in her home, which was divided into the part where she lived and the part where she taught. Every time I went, at midday, she would make me scrambled eggs and toast—my first experience of scrambled eggs—and then we'd go into her big studio with long windows that looked out on the garden. On those wintry London days with Ada, the sun never came out; it was always cold, and the trees in her garden were bare.

She told me that acting consisted of two things, tension and release. Or, as she would say, "You build, build, build . . . you inhale, inhale, inhale . . . and then you release . . . exhale, exhale, exhale." Every speech, she said, is releasing something that has been building inside; the words are the release of the emotional state. She had me practice by running across the room to the opposite wall, then pausing, holding my breath, exhaling, and then finally speaking. We did this over and over again. Well, at that point in my life I would have tried anything to prove that I had a talent buried somewhere inside of me! But it felt like every time I ran toward the wall I was also hitting a wall. It was very mechanical; my expression was all bottled up and refused to come out. Ada gave me a speech of Nina's from the Chekhov play *The Seagull,* and she had me run to the wall, build, build, build the tension, then release it to say my line: "I'm a seagull. No, that's not it. I'm an actress." It was horrible. I didn't feel like a seagull, and I didn't feel like an actress. The monologue sounded flat and lifeless, and I felt hopeless.

Finally, after a dozen of these scrambled-egg sessions, Ada sat me down at her breakfast table. "My dear Agapi," she said, "you are a wonderful girl and truly a wonderful human being. But you are not an actress, and it's better I tell you now so you don't waste your time trying."

Of course I believed her. Why wouldn't I? I had no other reference point either inside or outside of myself. That was the bad news. As it turned out, there was good news, too. Ada was going back to America to run the American Academy of Dramatic Arts in New York, but there was another teacher I could see, who taught and also directed at RADA. "I'll tell her about you," Ada said. "Maybe she can teach you what I haven't been able to."

How amazing of her, I thought. *She believes I am not an actress, but she is willing to introduce me to someone else anyway.* That was synchronicity at work again, using Ada to connect me with the right person. I didn't even have time to get discouraged, because one week later I was at Dunlop Studios for my first lesson with Eve Shapiro.

Born in South Africa, Eve was warm and energetic, and full of a passion for the theater that matched my own buried passion. It was love at first sight: no scrambled eggs, no toast, no big windows in her little studio in the Strand, where actors and musicians practice their craft. She gave me a play, *The Rose Tattoo* by Tennessee Williams, and told me to read the part of Serafina, the Italian-American widow who had lost the husband she adored and now faced rumors that he had had another woman in his life: the ultimate betrayal. I had many references from Greek plays and from my own mother's life, so I was in familiar territory. "Walk around like her," Eve suggested. "Think—what would she wear, what would she eat, how does she bathe? For the next week, be this woman. Feel the heat in her body and the passion in her heart. Let this woman speak to you, Agapi, and then let her come through you." Eve was speaking directly to the innate actress in me, and that actress knew what to do. No more inhale and exhale, no more tension and release, no more running to the wall. She was unleashing my creativity.

The next week, we went back—me and Serafina. I had her. Beyond the lines, beyond any analysis, she was alive in me. I did the monologue, from a scene where the priest comes to confront Serafina about how she has let herself go, walking around barefoot all the time, and she says he must tell her whether the rumors about her husband are true. Otherwise she'll go mad. In the little studio, I opened myself up and Serafina moved and spoke through me. I felt alive, I felt awake, and it was the most thrilling, wonderful feeling I had ever felt in my tender 17 years. Eve sat silently, taking in what had she had witnessed. Then she beamed, and her wave of happiness touched my heart. "Oh, Agapi," she said, "if they don't take you at RADA, there is something wrong with them, not with you."

What a seal of approval, what a source of confidence for a young girl about to audition for one of the best drama schools in the world! I felt like I had hit a home run. Eve and I worked diligently for the next few months, preparing the Serafina speech and another audition piece, a comedic monologue of Viola's in *Twelfth Night*. She was showing me how to have fun, trust my instincts, and get out of my own way.

When it was finally time to audition, my mother came with me. In spite of the work I had done with Eve, I was beyond nervous—my body was tense all over, my stomach in my throat, my voice so constricted that I wondered how I was going to express any emotion at all. We were almost an hour early, so my mother said, "Let's go to the pub!" She knew she had to do *something* if I was going to breathe any life into my Serafina or my Viola. We went to a pub nearby, and my mother ordered two Guinnesses, one for her and one for me.

There's something about a Guinness: the froth and the deep, sweet taste are very different from an ordinary beer. As I drank it, I relaxed and began to feel I could do anything. After all, if my mother was giving me a Guinness at the pub, it must be all right to loosen up a little! I went into my audition in full confidence, letting my exuberance spill out. In front of a panel of four teachers plus the principal, the wonderful Hugh Cruttwell, I gave it everything I had, and I had a ball. I was called back almost immediately, and a few days later they asked me in to interview with Mr. Cruttwell. He said to me, "You probably think you're a Greek tragedienne, but when you did your speech from *Twelfth Night,* I saw a real comedian in you." That must have been the Guinness!

The principal talked about parts that would be good for me to play in drama school, asking me if I was interested in Elektra or any of the other Greek heroines. He was hinting that I would get in, but of course he couldn't say that. Three more months passed—an agonizing wait—before I heard. One happy morning, I was in the shower washing my hair when my mother flung open the door and read, "It is with great pleasure that we announce to you that you have been accepted—"

She barely got to finish the letter. I screamed and I cried, hugging her and kissing her. I was the happiest girl in London!

And Eve Shapiro will forever stay in my heart as a landmark on my path—the perfect example of how a teacher can shape your destiny by giving you a safe space to bring forth what's inside you. She was the woman who saw beyond the closed door and gave me the chance to say, *This is who I am.*

CHAPTER 6

THE
SWAN

The story of how I moved from London to Los Angeles reads like a movie script, although it might be too far-fetched even for the silver screen. I was 22 years old, a recent graduate from the Royal Academy of Dramatic Art, and trying to figure out my next step in life. I had been going to auditions and playing small parts in fringe theater productions. Then, on a rare sunny English morning, my sister called me from L.A. She had been on tour to promote her first book, which had just hit the bestseller list.

My sister told me that at one of the gatherings for her book, she had met a Greek American businessman, a timber magnate from Colorado, and they had talked about me and my career aspirations. He was financing a Hollywood movie and had offered to consider me for the lead, and even to fly me over for the audition. My first reaction was elation mixed with disbelief—but before I had the time to respond, she said, "Nick is here with me now. I'm going to put him on."

The next thing I knew, I was hearing a man's voice with a heavy American accent. "A-gaa-pi, your sister tells me you're a wonderful actress. Are you a wonderful actress?"

"I am," I said, since I believed that I was. My mother had always counseled us against false modesty.

"Well, how would you like to come to Los Angeles and audition for this movie I'm producing?"

"I would love to."

"Okay, then I'm sending you a first-class ticket on TWA. Have you ever been to Los Angeles before?"

"No," I replied.

"Well, pack your bags. You're coming in two weeks."

"That's wonderful" was all I could manage to say. "Thank you so much."

When I put the phone down, I felt like I'd been hit by what the French call a *coup de foudre*—a bolt from the blue that had the potential to change my life. I told my mother, who reacted with delight, not at all surprised. It made perfect sense to her that something like this would happen; it was one of her beliefs, after all, that when you expect the unexpected, interesting things happen.

For the next two weeks I was restless with anticipation. Some of my friends gave me a farewell party at a Greek restaurant, and a notable English actor was there. He knew about Hollywood promises, so he took my hand and said, "My dear girl, I want you to know that if this doesn't work out, we will still love you and still be your friends, so you must come back to us." *He doesn't know what he's talking about,* I thought giddily. I was in my own bubble, and nobody was going to burst it.

In two weeks, as promised, I was sitting in first class on a TWA flight to Los Angeles. I felt like a star about to be discovered, well groomed in my carefully chosen red-and-white striped suit. My seatmate was the writer of a well-known TV series, and during the course of the flight I told him my story. I'm sure he must have thought, *Oh my God, does this girl know what she's in for?*

Nick had sent me the script of the film before I left. It was the story of a young European girl who comes to Hollywood and gets discovered. Her delicate beauty earns her the nickname "the Swan," and her name becomes a brand sponsoring cosmetics, bags, accessories, and many other products. In her swift rise to the top, however, she loses her sense of herself and has a nervous breakdown. A photographer, while taking her pictures, sees her fragility and falls in love with her. He comes to her rescue and manages to get her out of the business—the quintessential Hollywood fairy tale. While I was reading the script on the plane, my new-found friend asked if he could take a look at it. He informed me that it needed a lot of work. At that time, I had no idea what made a good script. "You are way too innocent for Hollywood," he said to me. Then he handed me his card and told me to keep him posted. As I arrived, I felt comforted by the thought that I had at least one friend in the city.

When I landed, a limo was waiting to take me to the Beverly Hills Hotel, where a huge bungalow had been reserved: a bedroom, a living room, and champagne on ice. There was a note from Nick that included his phone number. I called right away to let him know that I had arrived safely. "Nick, I'm here, and I'd love to meet you," I said. "When are you coming to town?" He said he didn't know, but the itinerary—including meeting the director, getting hair and makeup done, having photographs taken, meeting agents, and doing a screen test—was already arranged. I was stunned when he said, "I am a very busy man, but I will get there at some point." I felt like Eliza Doolittle without my Mr. Higgins.

I called my mother and sister to tell them that I had arrived safely in Hollywood-land and would keep them posted. Then I fell into a jet-lagged sleep, to be awakened in the morning by a call from the director's assistant, who wanted to book me for lunch with him that day at the Polo Lounge. I felt as if I'd landed on Mars. About an hour later there was a knock at the door. Thankfully, Howard, my friend from the plane, had come to see how this innocent young Greek girl was doing on her first day in Hollywood. I needed to see a familiar face. He joined me for breakfast, and things started to seem a little less surreal.

At lunch, I met the director and his wife. We discussed the script changes they were planning and how they envisioned the role, and they informed me that the next day I was scheduled to have my hair and makeup done and do a photo shoot. After another week of lunches and meetings with the full Hollywood cast of characters, I finally auditioned for the role of the Swan. Everything was happening so fast, and everybody seemed to be very happy with me, but I still hadn't met my mysterious benefactor, Nick.

Then one day he showed up and took me to dinner at La Scala. Nick stood six foot two, and he had strong, chiseled Greek features with black hair silvering at the temples. He looked as if he had just stepped off Mount Olympus, like one of the Greek gods. I remember being very nervous and not knowing quite what to think of him; he was larger than life, and I didn't have the faintest idea why he was being so generous when he had only met my sister twice. I also didn't know if I was living up to his expectations—was I good enough? But Nick said that the director was very happy with me, that everything was moving along beautifully, and they were just getting the rest of the financing in place.

The evening was an interesting clash of cultures. I kept telling him how much I loved people, and he would sternly reprimand me, saying, "A-gaa-pi, you cannot love people in Hollywood."

I felt like I was watching *myself* in a movie. I was connecting with all sorts of people who were inviting me to all sorts of places. As the weeks passed while we waited for the project to be green-lighted, I was enjoying myself—swimming, sunbathing, and playing tennis. It was an unexpected bonus when I met a well-known television actor and we fell in love. He and I had a wonderful connection, and we spent a lot of time at his little beach house a short drive down the coast. He preferred macrobiotic meals, which was new for me, but I was so smitten that I didn't even mind brown rice and steamed vegetables for breakfast instead of my usual croissant!

Into the second month of my stay, Nick was still paying all my expenses, including the Beverly Hills Hotel bungalow, plus a per diem. I'm sure people thought I was a kept woman; who would have believed the truth, that I was there to make a movie but I'd seen my benefactor only twice and could hardly ever get him on the phone?

I saw Nick once or twice more, but everything about the movie was beginning to sound tenuous. I decided to take acting classes with a local group to keep up my craft, and I continued to see friends, but now I was missing my family and my London life terribly. My relationship with the actor had fizzled out by now, and I felt displaced: I was meeting too many new people, there was no focus on the movie, and it looked as if my dream was falling apart.

I reached out to one of my new friends and confided my misgivings. She suggested that I join her for a yoga class led by the acclaimed teacher Bikram, who happened to be teaching a few blocks away from me. My mother had introduced me to yoga when I was 12, so it felt natural for me to pick it up again. I attended two classes a day, four hours in all, and the intensity was exhilarating. Bikram took an interest in me and became a wonderful friend and guide in what was turning into a very uncertain time.

I embarked on a fervent search. I would spend hours in Hollywood's metaphysical bookstore, the Bodhi Tree, picking up books on Ayurvedic science and Indian philosophy, and reading about the masters' experiences of cosmic consciousness and enlightenment. I didn't personally believe in the existence of God. I'd never really given it much thought. In my family, we always celebrated the holidays of the Greek Orthodox faith, Easter and Christmas, and my father was a believer in his own way, but my mother's true religion was communion with people and with life, and she raised us on metaphysics rather than dogma. I blindly called myself an agnostic and an existentialist, yet I yearned for connection to something greater than myself. It was as if I was walking around knocking on doors, having no idea which one might open.

One morning after my class with Bikram, I stopped in at the Bodhi Tree and spotted Paramahansa Yogananda's *Autobiography of a Yogi,* the book my mother had kept on her bedside table when she introduced us to yoga in Athens. I bought it and began devouring it! I spent many hours a day reading it, stopping to attend yoga class, then reading some more. The book, a spiritual classic if ever there was one, tells amazing stories of yogis in the Himalayas who live for hundreds of years: their bodies, connected through the breath to the Spirit, transcend physical reality, entering into the dimension of soul. Something deep inside of me was reawakening, remembering that there was another reality beyond Hollywood. I was realizing that I wasn't just this girl who had come to America to find her destiny in acting; I was part of a much larger whole. I was not just my physical body and my personality, my wants and ambitions, my ups and downs in life. I was reminded of the existence of my soul.

I'll never forget the morning when I was awakened very early by sunlight coming through my window. As I rose from my bed, I felt myself illumined by an outer light and at the same time flooded by an inner light. I fell to my knees and started to weep, the tears rolling down my face. They were the tears of my soul being awakened. I called out, "Father, Father, Father," connecting with my Maker as if for the first time, and every time I said it I felt a jolt of energy in my spine. A few minutes later, I opened my diary and wrote simply, *Credo.* An ancient memory and promise was being revealed: *I believe, I know, I am a child of God.* That moment would forever change me. A door had opened and the light had come in.

The next morning, Nick called me and said in a matter-of-fact tone that the movie was not going forward. The financing had fallen through. He said I was free to use my return ticket and return to London.

I wanted to say to him, "Nick, I know now why you brought me here and who sent you to me." But instead I said, "I don't know how I will ever be able to thank you for all that you have done for me. I am not going to be using my ticket right now." I put the phone down with a smile.

I looked at my plane ticket lying there on the coffee table in front of me. It represented a known destination. However, I now wanted to travel the unknown path.

A few days later, I moved in with some friends in the Hollywood Hills, beginning my quest. My goal was no longer just to have an acting career, but to explore this new awakening. *The Swan* might have been no more, but I was taking flight.

CHAPTER 7

GOLDEN DOORS

After the film for which I had come to Los Angeles fell through, I had a choice. I was free to go back to London. I had my return ticket, prepaid. I didn't know what was ahead of me, but I decided not to return. Remembering a story that my mother used to tell me and my sister when we were young, I stepped beyond my fears and followed what I knew in my heart was right—and I'm so glad I did.

My mother had joined the Greek Red Cross as a nurse when the Second World War broke out. She had a passion for contributing and making a difference wherever she could, and she went with a willing heart to do whatever it took. She just couldn't bear to sit idly by, especially since she had some basic medical training.

In the mid-1940s, as the conflict in Greece shifted into civil war, she and a group of nurses were sent into the mountains in the north. There, in the remote cabin where they tended the wounded, they were also sheltering two Jewish girls in flight from the Nazis and their Greek collaborators. One night my mother was sitting combing her hair—she had long, beautiful auburn hair—when three German soldiers burst in with their guns and opened fire, shouting orders to give up the Jews they were hiding. The woman next to her was hit and fell to the ground. In an instant, without a thought for what might happen to her, my mother rose up and in fluent German said, "Put your guns down! You have no right to shoot—we are Red Cross!" In the next instant she saw the three Germans lower their guns.

It all happened in a moment, but it was a moment that opened a door inside her to find a courage that would carry her through the rest of her life. Faced with life's daunting challenges—marrying my father, whose infidelities would shake her to her core; daring to leave him without having any independent means of support; wanting the best quality of life for her daughters, but not always knowing where those means would come from; even just making ends meet—she would recall the experience in the mountains and think, *I am the woman who told three German soldiers to put down their guns, and they did. If I can do that, I can do anything.*

There's a wonderful pair of lines in a poem by Emily Dickinson: *We never know how high we are / Till we are asked to rise.* That's exactly what was being asked of my mother in the cabin in the mountains. She was being asked to rise above her natural fear and her perceived human limitations to do something she never imagined she could.

It's no accident that we speak of "rising to a challenge." That's exactly what happens when we face fear: we transcend our limits and we show ourselves what we're truly capable of. And we may find, to our amazement, that we can rise higher than we ever dreamed possible. My mother's ability to stand up and take charge gave her a sense of her own indomitable spirit. Her fearlessness reached such a height in that encounter with the Germans that when her comb fell on the floor, and one of the soldiers picked it up, she said to him, "May I please have my comb back? I think I need it more than you do!"

Throughout her life, my mother was asked over and over again to open closed doors. When she brought my sister and me from Athens to London to be educated, when she came with us to America to live, she stayed true to her vision of what she believed was possible for us. At every step, she was leaving familiar ground—safe ground—fearlessly reaching for a farther horizon.

As we grew up, my mother would often tell us about that morning in the cabin and the soldiers who dropped their guns on her command. She would remind us of the power that had made it possible for her to do that. She used to say to us, "When you have looked down the barrels of three machine guns, and you see those guns lower because you told them so, you discover the tremendous power that lies within you."

Now, in the midst of all my fears, that same strength was carrying me forward. I thought, *I am the daughter of the mother who did that. Maybe I, too, can do anything.*

There were many more doors to open, and they were going to open in the most natural way, in perfect timing. They weren't necessarily going to be the acting doors. But the doors to myself were unlocking.

I made the decision to immerse myself in my spiritual life. I found a spiritual teacher who spoke to my heart. I started meditating, going to seminars, and educating myself about the lives of masters on the path. I created a safe haven for myself. Out of all the men I was meeting, I chose to be with a lovely man with whom I felt very secure. I wasn't in love with him, but we cared deeply for each other. We moved in together and made our home into a sanctuary where I cooked for friends and we brought a feeling of family into our lives. He taught me how to drive, and I taught him how to vacuum. All this time, I was committing myself to the spiritual path I had chosen. I wasn't just going outside myself, as I had done when I sought acting jobs; now I was going inside myself, to seek Agapi, whom I didn't really know.

I wasn't comfortable; my path was uncertain, sometimes painful. But they were growing pains. As I learned to live in the uncertainty and the unknown, the ray of light that had illumined me that day in my hotel room kept gently ushering me forward. I released all the angst over the acting career, the pressure of trying to make that dream happen. It was a huge letting go.

In the midst of all the unknown, the insecurity over not knowing what was going to happen next and how it was all going to turn out, and all these questions in my young life, there was a hope rising inside me. It was the hope that something wonderful was going to hap-

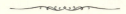

pen. I was the daughter of a woman who had seen three machine guns go down because she told them so. That same light that had been in her was now igniting me, awakening little by little, and it needed a safe haven in which to grow strong. It needed tending to, so that it could light up my life—and then light up other people's lives as well.

CHAPTER 8

SAINT JOAN
ON THE BUS

When I graduated from RADA, I had thought my contract with success was signed. I'd expected that all doors would open automatically for me. My thinking went something like this: *I have just finished attending one of the best drama schools in the world. I have been told I am very talented. I have been acknowledged as a gifted actress by my teachers and my peers. Basically, I should walk into any audition and people should recognize my talent and hire me on the spot. Why wouldn't they?* That was the planet I was living on. There were not many other inhabitants.

As I shared with you in an earlier chapter, fate had pulled me out of London to go to Hollywood and make a movie, but it seemed as if the gods had played a trick on me. Isn't it often the case that we go after one thing, only to find out that it's a disguise for something much more essential to our lives?

I stayed in Los Angeles, pursuing the acting profession on my own while also pursuing my inner growth. I went on auditions, and I kept being told how gifted I was. But it didn't translate into jobs, and for a long time I felt very stuck. Apart from some small theater parts, Hollywood wasn't getting me—which makes sense, because I hadn't gotten me either. Casting directors would say to me, "You're so great, but we don't know what to do with you because . . . " Fill in the blank: "You are too young" or "You are too old" or "You are too short" or "You are too tall" or "You have an accent" or simply "You don't fit in with the rest of the cast." There was always something! I just didn't fit in.

I was walking around the world constantly wanting something, finding that the world wasn't giving it to me and having no idea how to even begin giving it to myself. It was painful and isolating, and it was starting to close off my self-expression—a very bad thing for a performer.

My whole identity was wrapped up in succeeding as an actress. When I went on an audition, I was very attached to the results. I think that acting is one of the hardest professions for that reason: you always have to put yourself out there 100 percent for your next job, every single time, and you have to live with rejection, even if you are at your best. So you need incredible self-esteem and self-acceptance, along with a tremendous capacity to handle disappointment—unless, of course, you've managed to have no expectations at all. And if you've managed that, you're probably no longer in the profession, but living in the Himalayas as a fully enlightened being!

Since I had not yet become a fully enlightened being, I kept at it. Years went by. I moved to New York with my mother and sister to try the theater, where I thought I might fit in better. I took classes with the celebrated acting teacher Uta Hagen, gaining more experience and solidifying my craft. Then I heard that the Williamstown Theatre Festival was casting for the six-hour play *The Greeks,* which was an adaptation of ten great Greek tragedies combined: *The Trojan Women* by Euripides, the *Oresteia* of Aeschylus, and others. I thought the text read like a poem, and I loved the material. I was convinced there would be something there for me.

So I went to audition for Nikos Psacharopoulos, the director of the Williamstown Theatre in Massachusetts, with a monologue from George Bernard Shaw's *Saint Joan.* I had a fantastic audition! Nikos directed me throughout it, and I was able to take all his notes and implement them on the spot. As I left, I felt great. I knew I had done my very best.

A week later, Nikos called me back. "My dear girl," he said, "I don't know what to do with you. You are so talented and so gifted, but you don't have a big enough name for me to give you the big parts of Elektra, Klytemnestra, Kassandra, or any others. And I can't stick you in the chorus—you have such a vibrant personality that you'll stick out. I'm sad to tell you that I can't really offer you anything."

I put the phone down and cried my eyes out. I remember going to my mother, sobbing, "I can't even get a part for six hours of *The Greeks!*" I was a Greek actress! Where else could I turn? What hope was there for me? And down the emotional rabbit hole I went. But it would lead to an epiphany I never expected.

One day during that time, I was riding the bus to my singing lesson on the Upper East Side of Manhattan when I started to notice the faces of the other passengers. Each one of them looked like a closed door: they seemed to be shut down, their worries and burdens the only things showing in their expressions. As I looked at the people around me, I was filled with compassion. I started to realize that others might have disappointments much bigger than mine. *If only I could bring some joy onto this bus,* I thought. And then I realized that I could. *I could act right here! I could entertain these people for a brief moment. I could do a song and dance right here and now!*

I had a gift for acting, for dramatic and emotional expression, but it was more than that; it was a gift for touching others with what I expressed. And with that thought, I broke down the barriers. I reached out to the woman next to me and asked her if she liked the theater. We started talking about our favorite plays and characters, and I told her that mine was *Saint Joan.* She knew the play, and we had an unexpectedly wonderful conversation. In my enthusiasm, I said to her, "Would you like me to do Joan's monologue for you?"

"I would love that," she said.

The first words are addressed to Joan's jurors, who have condemned her to life in prison, telling her they are doing it to spare her life; in this scene, she chooses to be burned at the stake instead. She says to them, "You promised me my life, but you lied. You think that life is nothing but not being stone dead . . ." As I said the words, the woman's face started to change. I could see that she was being touched; I was being touched as well, remembering a promise I had made to myself.

By the time I finished, the woman on the bus had tears in her eyes. As she got off at her stop, she thanked me. I felt elated. I felt a release, as if a door had opened that I didn't even know was there. Here I was thinking I was this exceptionally gifted girl who was not being recognized by the world. And then it dawned on me what conditions I had put on my gift. My promise to myself was not to become a famous actress, it was to live up to my name—*Agapi,* unconditional love. I saw that the real promise of my life was to give unconditionally, not just on the stage, but on the bus, or wherever I might find myself, today or in years to come. The promise was to share my gifts and let nothing stand between the world and my love.

CHAPTER 9

BATH TIME

I was 12 when my parents separated, and my mother, sister, and I moved from the large apartment where we'd lived with my father into a smaller apartment in Athens.

It happened so suddenly. It was the middle of September, just before school was to start. My mother had decided to leave my father and had confronted him during our family vacation outside Athens. I didn't quite know what was happening, so at the end of our vacation I was stunned to be driven to a new apartment instead of returning home. When I asked my mother why we were going there, I could sense her unease as she told me that we were going to live away from our father for a while. In the myth of Persephone, the goddess of spring, there is a distinct moment when the earth splits under her feet and Hades, the god of the underworld, comes up and abducts her. The earth closes above her, leaving her trapped in the underworld. The moment my mother told me the news, I felt exactly like that. The ground had opened beneath my feet and I was free-falling. I began to look back, trying to grasp the enormity of the change and figure out how I could have prevented it, as if I had been responsible for what had happened.

I adored my father and I knew how much he loved me. Bringing him happiness had been one of my life's joys. I had ways to draw him out of his preoccupations and make him laugh with my playfulness and whimsical observations. Visiting my father now was extremely difficult because the separation was not something he had initiated. He was wounded and angry. Underneath the extraordinary love and caring with which my mother was now beginning to raise us on her own, I could feel her pain and sorrow too. The hearts of the two people whom I loved so much were bound by the unspoken grief of separation.

I had no way to even begin to vocalize my feelings. How could I? I was only 12. Perhaps because I had a flair for the dramatic, I created a fictional character, as children often do, to help me cope: an imaginary friend called Anna. Anna was the perfect girl. She was so together, she was so independent, she was smart and in control. She was an amazing creature. She kept me company and talked to me endlessly about how I should act. Anna, in her perfection, was my defense mechanism— the ideal cover-up for the insecurity and vulnerability that I was feeling. She kept me steady, and I looked to her for the confidence I was missing.

Another way I coped was by attracting friends who sought comfort, who needed someone to talk to about their problems. The comfort I could not give myself, I was now giving to others, hoping that some of it would be returned to me. And it was. I felt needed and valued. That, of course, would develop into a lifelong pattern. On some level, I held on to the belief that vulnerability was risky and that perfection could protect me against my pain.

Twenty years after that wrenching separation, life had gone on, much had transpired, and I was living in New York in a tiny apartment on the fourth floor of a townhouse where the bed literally took up the whole bedroom—but it was a cozy, safe haven. A producer friend of mine had helped put me on the track of producing, which I found invigorating. I was now using all my creative skills, and I felt more in charge and in control. I was developing and trying to produce a documentary for television, and I had a fantastic script and a great director; all I was missing was the money. I reached out to foundations, corporations, and private investors to see who would fund the project. I had a lot of hurdles to overcome, but I kept putting one foot in front of the other, bypassing all my personal insecurities. The trouble was that in the process of trying to raise funds, I was totally missing the fun! It became all-consuming, to the point that when people asked me, "How are you?" I would respond by telling them how my fund-raising was going. It was as though the project and I had merged.

At the same time, strangely, I was feeling disconnected from myself and rather alone. I was pursuing my master's degree in spiritual psychology, and I was doing a lot of healing inner work, but I had the nagging sense that some part of me was being left behind while my warrior-self marched ahead, toward my goal. Walking around with a knot in my stomach became normal.

One Sunday evening, I was traveling home from Philadelphia, where I was taking the master's degree course. While I was on the train, I began reflecting on the work we'd done that weekend, accessing neglected parts of ourselves. When I got home, I drew a bath, and there in a moment of relaxation while immersed in the water, I felt the presence of a young girl—vulnerable and open, a child waiting to be taken in. I realized I knew this person—of course! I had known her all my life. I just hadn't talked to her in a very long time. She had been buried underneath the self that had grown up, and there she had remained, trapped by the fear that she was alone in the world.

This part of myself was very familiar to me—her shape, her look, and an inherent innocence that I knew so well. She wasn't Anna, my impossibly perfected alter ego; she was the part that had been exiled in the underworld while the rest of me was being educated, living, and working. Frightened and insecure, she could find no room in the world I was creating for myself. She had made the decision that the world was not a safe place. There was no one there to comfort her. Her voice was silenced. She felt her magic was gone. It was as if she'd been evicted, but never really left home, just waited outside the closed door. I was humbled and moved that she had decided to make her presence known to me. I felt her loneliness, and my heart leaped to her out of love for this part that had been hurting all these years. No wonder I had been walking around feeling disconnected from myself. No wonder I had felt so alone.

From that moment on, I made a promise that I would not abandon her again. I took her fully into my heart. I checked in with her regularly and listened to what she had to say. She told me what she liked and what she didn't like, whom she felt safe with and whom she didn't trust, what made her feel alive. She told me when her feelings were hurt and what brought her joy, and I listened to it all and brought my wisdom and compassion to her. It was powerful to see how, just by expressing something I had suppressed—a feeling of loneliness or anxiety or insecurity—I could make room for the feeling to release its hold on me. Waves of happiness started to fill the places of disconnection, making me realize for the first time that happiness really resides in knowing, accepting, and loving ourselves.

This was a moment worth celebrating. There was this ring I loved, made by a jeweler friend, a pearl nestled with three small diamonds in a gold-embossed band. I decided that I would buy it as a symbol of the bond with my newfound self. I bought the ring, and when I put it on, I lit up inside.

A month or so later, a friend and I went to see the ballet *Swan Lake,* which happened to be my favorite; I'd danced in it when I was a child in Greece, and the music had stirred my heart ever since. As we took our seats, the orchestra was tuning up and the curtain was open, revealing the mist of the lake drifting over the stage. On impulse, I turned to my friend and said, "Would you do a blessing on me with my ring?" And right there in the balcony, in front of the misty, magical Swan Lake, I made a vow to that newfound part of me, for better or for worse, to walk the whole journey together.

After that, I made sure never to go out without putting my pearl ring on. It was a constant reminder that when I went out into the world, all of me was coming with me, under my protection. Because I was so much more confident and connected to myself, I could connect with other people in a more authentic way, and my relationships became richer. As I interacted with people, I found myself becoming more aware of their neglected and abandoned parts too. I think that the isolation so many people experience is a result of that same separation from parts of themselves that have been disowned.

We feel that in order to function in the world, we have to put aside some deeply imperfect, human part of ourselves. But ultimately, the only way to make these parts perfect is to accept them with love and compassion. To be more fulfilled and at peace within ourselves, we have to restore all parts of us and welcome them home. The world can only seem a safe place when we feel safe inside.

CHAPTER 10

KEEP GOING ON AT ALL COSTS

Have you ever seen the Greek movie *Never on Sunday*? It's the story of a hooker who never works on Sundays and an intellectual writer who falls in love with her and tries to transform her. But in the end she actually frees *him* from being stuck in his head and helps him find the joy of life.

The movie became a musical, and it was produced at a small theater in Hollywood. By now I was living in Los Angeles again—I moved from one coast to the other and back a number of times in these years—but my identity was no longer so tightly bound up in being an actress, and I was beginning to find my own joy in life. I was able to act just for the love of it—and, perhaps because I had made room for them, the opportunities found me. I auditioned for *Never on Sunday* and I was offered the part of the best friend of the lead, a girl named Mando. There was no pay for the show, but I was so happy to be acting that I would have paid large sums of money for the opportunity.

The cast was mostly Greek Americans, and the director was a woman who had what are politely called "personality issues." She had a powerful gift for alienating every single person in the cast. Even though she was known to be a talented director, she came across as tyrannical, opinionated, and a bully.

We were rehearsing in Glendale, outside Los Angeles. The director would call rehearsals for 4 P.M., right at the height of rush hour. My scenes were not being rehearsed until 6 or 7 P.M., so I would say to her, "I'd like to come at five-thirty so I can avoid the traffic." To which she would reply: "I want the whole cast here at four, and if you don't want to come, I can replace you. I have people waiting in line for your part."

That was her tone most of the time at rehearsal. I wanted to either quit, let her have it, or have someone kidnap her so we'd get a different director—not unlike the way I used to wish my math teacher would die. And this sentiment was shared by all. I was struggling to do the best I could in my acting and manage my feelings about her. People kept advising me to ignore her, which was a great idea—in theory. My sister kept telling me to see her as a character in a play. But every time she did something, my blood boiled, and I could literally feel my temperature rising in unison with my anger level.

One night I was having dinner with some friends and my spiritual teacher. We were all sitting around the table, talking and enjoying ourselves, and I decided to ask my teacher for advice. I explained the situation—how unreasonable the director was, how furious she made me—and asked him what he thought I should do. He took one of the paper napkins and on it he wrote: KEEP GOING ON AT ALL COSTS.

I got it, just like that. I had no choice. So my lesson was to use the energy of the conflict as fuel for my performance. I told myself, *If I think I'm having a hard time, how about Mando?* She *has a hard life! If she's not letting the circumstances of her life bring her down, neither will I.* So I poured all that energy into my love for my character, and my heart went out to her. I drove to Glendale during rush hour listening to lively Greek music and love songs. My director's difficult ways were not going to get to me anymore.

We opened the play, and despite all the friction and ill will she'd created, there was a full house, and I was thriving in my role. It was as if all that thorny, biting energy had become grist for the mill of my creativity. I was having a ball!

But wait . . . there's more. Every night at the end of the play, we had to strike the set because the space was used for a class the next day. I usually wanted to go out with friends who'd come to see the show. But our director's rules stated that I—all of us—had to stay and take the set down, when we all knew that for a few dollars she could have hired help to do all that. I found myself, once again, rebelling—sometimes even storming out and refusing to take part.

One night, she informed me that my job that evening was to clean the bathrooms: empty the trash cans, wipe the sinks, stock paper goods, and so on. You might think that would have been the last straw. But something happened to me that night that I'll never forget.

I started humming while cleaning the bathrooms! I felt no resistance at all. It was a total surrender. I thought to myself, *Well, if that's what needs to be done, I'll be a happy cleaner.*

I was enjoying myself so much that I went on to clean the seats in the theater. I felt I could have also cleaned the street outside, and the whole city of Los Angeles too. My ego had stopped fighting her—stopped judging the task as stupid and her as mean. All those judgments were suspended, and in that moment, I was free.

The director came up to me and said, "Agapi! What are you doing? Stop, you've done enough!" She thanked me for all the good work and acknowledged me for my performance, and her eyes teared up. I remember driving home relaxed and yet elated. I felt myself smiling as I realized how the whole experience had been a setup for me to find my freedom and unbind the ego-strings around my heart.

While I was doing the play, I had auditioned for James Ivory, who was directing the film *Surviving Picasso*, with Anthony Hopkins in the role of Picasso. The day after *Never on Sunday* closed, I got a call from Ivory's office offering me the part of the maid to Hopkins's Picasso, with fun scenes like bringing him breakfast in bed and going grocery shopping for him in the Paris markets. So I had graduated to my next assignment. I might be playing the maid, but at least I was working with Anthony Hopkins in Paris!

As wonderful as it was to be working with such masters in the field, and as grateful as I was for the opportunity, I still had to deal with the part of myself that really wanted to be the leading lady. To enjoy the experience for what it was and extract its real goodness, I had to realize that I was the leading lady in my own life, no matter what I was doing, whether I was cleaning a bathroom, playing a maid, writing a book, or making baklava. Whether or not I had my name in lights, I had to focus on filling that crucial role inside myself.

CHAPTER 11

THE INVISIBLE MAPQUEST

Greek mythology didn't interest me at all when I was at school. I found the stories unrealistic and rather dull, and irrelevant to my life. I loved real characters in plays, but the characters of Greek mythology left me completely cold. The gods didn't spark any creativity, or anything at all, in me. But unbeknownst to me, they had a plan, and I was part of it!

When I was 16, my mother gave me a volume of Carl Jung's writings translated into English, called *The Archetypes and the Collective Unconscious,* which traces the roots of the Greek myths and other legends deep in the human psyche. I was reading it, although I could hardly understand it, and it must have been sinking into my unconscious, setting the direction for one of the most joyful, meaningful, creative chapters of my life.

Years later, when I lived in Los Angeles, I was quest-ing for a way to give expression to my talent and my passion. I embarked on a program of study that led me to profound transformation. It was a master's program designed to help people find their life's purpose and calling, claim their gifts, and clear the path to mak-ing a meaningful contribution in the world. The first year dealt with the healing of old beliefs, distorted self-images, and painful stored-up memories. During that time, I came face-to-face with my hidden insecurities, my habit of comparing myself to others, and the way I dealt with hurt by shutting down. I was preparing a new foundation to build on.

In the second year of the program, students are re-quired to do a project that realizes a long-held dream—anything from writing a novel or opening a restaurant to traveling abroad, finding true love, or even having a child. I knew that my project would have something to do with theater; I just didn't know what form it would take.

Funnily enough, one of the books on the syllabus was that very same book of Jung that my mother had given me. This time, as I read it, I started to understand the significance these archetypes have in our lives. At the same time, I was also reading Joseph Campbell's book *The Power of Myth,* and it all started to connect—the sto-ries, the gods, and our human lives. I began to research the stories and the figures in greater depth, especially the feminine archetypes. But I still hadn't found a subject for my project.

By now my sister was married, with two young daughters, living in Santa Barbara, and my mother was living with them. One night we were all gathered in their kitchen—our family haven—with several women friends who had joined us for a dinner prepared by my mother. We were enjoying the conversation over wine and Greek food, all having a really good time. Looking around the table, I suddenly realized that I saw all the different Greek-goddess archetypes sitting right there with me. One friend was married and had totally embraced the role of wife—Hera; one was a sensual, exuberant woman who was never without a man, but rarely the same man—Aphrodite; another was the consummate career woman, my lawyer friend—Athena. There was our outdoorsy friend, straight off the ranch, who loved nature and her horses more than anything—Artemis. There was the one who was always at some spiritual retreat or other, involved in some philanthropic cause, saving humanity—that was Hestia; and there was the ultimate Demeter, my mother, feeding everyone and taking care of us all. And I was like Persephone, the goddess of spring, closely bonded with her mother and intensely absorbed in her journey of transformation. I watched all these colorful characters in front of me as if I were looking into a kaleidoscope, seeing the beautiful pieces of a pattern always moving and changing. All the different women sitting around the table, telling their stories— these were the real goddesses!

As I lay in bed that night, still energized by the experience, I started to think how wonderful it would be to put these women in a play, telling their stories. But that seemed impractical, because they all had their own lives, and they were not actresses! So I thought, *I'll gather a few actresses to play the parts of the different goddesses.* But then I realized that all these aspects, all these archetypes, live in every woman. So what if one woman were to play all the parts? And that's how my one-woman show was born: *Conversations with the Goddesses.*

I decided I would create a script with stories told by a narrator and monologues that gave each goddess her own voice. As I thought about what I wanted these women to say, I went back to the plays and characters I had seen and studied at the Royal Academy, and I realized that those different characters embodied the distinct personalities of the goddesses, too. So I decided to give each goddess a monologue from one of the plays I had acted in and so loved: Shakespeare, Bernard Shaw, Tom Stoppard, Tennessee Williams, Eugene O'Neill, the Greeks—they were all there, with all their great speeches in the different voices of women.

For the first time in a very long time, I felt I was now on the right track. I was filled with excitement and anticipation as I put the pieces together, writing the framing narrative to tell the goddesses' stories and giving them voice through the monologues. When it came time to produce the show, it was amazing how the doors started to open. I was talking about the project to a friend in Los Angeles who owned a gallery, and he offered me his space for the performance. Friends caught the spark and offered to help me design the set like a temple; some offered to bring the food for the celebration after the performance; others provided the music and assisted in any way they could. The word went out, and we had a full house. I told the stories; the characters came alive. The goddesses I couldn't care less about in eighth grade had now come to my aid to help me on my creative path. Ultimately, they would usher me to all the right people and places so that they could be seen. Sometimes I felt like their puppet! But it was all working to my advantage, so I wasn't complaining.

A friend who was the curator of the Getty Villa in Los Angeles was in the audience at the gallery, and he had the idea to bring the show to that wonderful museum of ancient art and culture, and stage it in front of the antiquities there. The performance came alive in a whole new way in that setting; as I told the stories in front of the ancient statues, the goddesses came down off their pedestals and into people's lives. A publisher happened to see a videotape of the show at the Getty and approached me to suggest a book on it. And it wasn't long after that before I had a contract to write my first book. The goddesses were pulling me down the path at full speed.

I've seen this now so many times with friends, family, and so many other people I've come in contact with. We set out to do one thing, then it turns out that the thing we're going after is not what we want after all. Something sacred and unseen is calling us underneath the surface, something that is uniquely ours to do. I think we're born with this—our own guidance system, our invisible MapQuest. It becomes visible to us at last when we start seeing not through the eyes of the world, from the perspective of what we should be doing or achieving or accomplishing, but with the eyes of truth, which see who we are and what we are here to do.

CHAPTER 12

FINDING
YOUR VOICE

When I began work on my first book, I was living on my own in a one-bedroom apartment in New York. I had entered a new territory, with a new sense of responsibility and commitment to myself and my work. After some initial excitement over getting a book contract, the honeymoon was over: there I was, alone, facing the unknown. I was filled with trepidation and unsure of how to say what I wanted to say—not even confident that I had anything original to say at all.

My voice was being held hostage by doubts, comparisons, and fears of rejection, not unlike the way I'd felt when I first started studying acting in London, finding my way uncertainly in a new field. I was struggling to put words on paper. Then, when the words did start to come, other voices would join the chorus, criticizing and judging. *Your ideas are too simplistic. You're not quali-fied to write a book about the archetypes. No one will listen to what you say.* All this cacophony was drowning out whatever truth wanted to be expressed.

In the middle of this uncertainty, quite unexpect-edly, a friend from out of town whom I hadn't seen in a long time called to ask if she could stay with me for the weekend while she attended a neuroscience seminar in the city. A very intense person, she came across as someone with a great deal of authority, always assum-ing she knew what was right for you. I was reluctant to say yes, but I decided to uphold my Greek tradition of hospitality.

The night my friend arrived, I shared the doubts and difficulties of my writing with her, and to my surprise, I found that she was listening to me without offering any advice. I kissed her good night and tucked her into bed in my living room. It was Friday night, and she had to leave early the next morning to go to her seminar. I was a bit surprised when she knocked on my bedroom door the next morning, while it was still barely light outside, asking me to wake up.

"I'm sleeping, darling," I called out. "Can we talk later?"

"No," she said urgently. "I have an insight about your book—a message from Spirit. It can't wait."

I thought, *You've got to be kidding me. Couldn't Spirit wait until I've had my morning coffee?* But, half asleep, I plopped down on the living-room sofa. At the time, I kept an easel with a pad of paper, on which I would note inspirations and ideas that came to me during the day. She placed the easel in front of me, thrust a marker into my hand, and said to me, "Write this down." Then she started dictating: *"I have everything I need to write this book. But I lack one thing: confidence. And the reason I lack confidence is that I think I am going to do it on my own. I am forgetting that I have inner support, inner allies, inner knowledge that comes from something beyond me. I am not alone. I already have the information in me, and I need to trust it. If I am open to receiving this assistance, all sorts of support will come my way."*

Oh, sweet Jesus, I thought to myself. There I was, half asleep, and she was channeling the Greek oracle at six o'clock in the morning.

She continued, and I wrote: *"My task is to be committed and not distract myself. I should keep a log of when I am distracted and when I am committed. That's the way I will build the muscle of my inner commitment."* She told me I had a pattern of seeking my fulfillment through other people, and the reason I was experiencing a challenge now was that I was being called to experience my own fulfillment, which was new for me. I was breaking a very deep, old habit.

She was right. I wrote it all down in red marker, every word. It was a catalytic moment, and I felt so alive that to this day I have saved that paper as a reminder that confidence and strength come from the knowledge that we are never alone.

After that, everything was different. My friend had helped me take the lid off my creativity, and, like the breakthrough I'd had in London with my acting teacher Eve Shapiro, the goddesses started to take over and speak through me. At last, the voice that was buried inside me was making itself heard. Thoughts, words, emotions, and ideas were now connecting and flooding through me. In coffee shops, at the gym, or with friends—everywhere I went, I heard the constant murmur of my creative voice. I had so much to say that I wrote wherever I was, sometimes on napkins or place mats if I didn't have my laptop. I'd gone from being a dry riverbed to being Niagara Falls!

When I finished the manuscript of my book, I put it in a blue binder, ready to send to my editor, and then I sat on the couch with the binder in my lap and cried. In my mind's eye I saw the seven goddesses walking down a staircase toward me, one by one, and I heard an inner voice say, "Your life will never be the same." And it was true. When the book was ready for release, my friend Deepak Chopra invited me to launch it with my one-woman show on the goddesses at his center. The show was received with great enthusiasm, and people lined up afterward for me to sign my book until we ran out of copies! My voice was finding resonance with others, and that was so fulfilling for me. And one of the great gifts was that my mother was there to witness the beginning of this new phase of my life. After all, she had been my lifelong inspiration as a woman who, throughout her life, had stood up without fear to speak her truth.

I remember when she decided to leave my father after enduring his infidelities for so many years. I was 12 years old. We were vacationing at a resort outside Athens when I suddenly heard shouting from the next room—extreme, volatile shouting, a voice raised in rage. It was my mother's voice, yelling at my father, telling him she'd had enough—she was going to leave him and take me and my sister with her.

My father was saying, "Don't shout! You're going to wake up the whole hotel!" And my mother yelled back, "I don't care if I wake up all of Athens!" There were so many odds against her: breaking from the conformity of a marriage and living on her own with two children was a very hard thing to do at that time. But she was finally speaking up and saying, *Enough!* She was expressing her truth without waiting for anyone's permission.

In that moment, I realized that it takes courage to express your voice and your truth. It doesn't always sound pretty. Sometimes it is awkward, but it deserves encouragement so that it can be heard. Each one of us has our own voice, our own truth to speak. It's uniquely ours—a ray of light trying to shine through the density of this material world. When we give it permission to speak without weighing the consequences—when we express what needs to be expressed, even if that isn't the "right" thing to say—it transforms our reality, because it shows us the way back to ourselves.

CHAPTER 13

REFRAMING SUCCESS

One of my dreams was to film my one-woman show, tied to my book about the goddesses, for PBS. Through a friend, I was introduced to a producer who loved the idea. His first e-mail to me had the subject line "Moving Forward with The Goddesses," and I knew I was in the right hands. From then on, as we e-mailed back and forth, all our e-mails were titled "Re: Moving Forward"—giving the project a sense of direction and momentum that propelled me along.

I gave all my energy and my full attention to producing this show. I poured into it 100 percent of my creativity and my passion. The performance was to be filmed in front of a live audience—a fully scripted theatrical piece for cameras, with a set fit for the goddesses. Though we had a small budget, we managed to find set and light-

ing designers, the perfect outdoor venue, and a wonderful studio audience that created an electric atmosphere.
We even found the perfect outfit for me—a gorgeous designer gown that had its own line in the budget!—and
a director who realized the vision perfectly. People came
from so many avenues to assist me in manifesting this
dream, and it turned the filming into a truly stellar experience. The producer thought it was going to be a smash
hit, bigger than anything he had done before.

But that's not how it turned out. When the special
aired, it was in the wrong place at the wrong time: a local PBS station in a very small niche market, literally in
the middle of the night, at 12 A.M. on a Saturday. It was a
bad time slot to test the market; viewership was very low,
and other stations took it as a sign. This caused a domino
effect, and in the end PBS picked up the special only
sporadically instead of giving it the wide release we had
hoped for. Everybody who saw it loved it, but in terms of
commercial success, it was a huge disappointment.

To have put in so much effort for so small a return
was hard to take. One day I was sitting at my desk, filled
with sadness and discouragement, asking myself for the
hundredth time if I had done something wrong. Then,
quite at random, an e-mail popped up in my in-box from
a name I didn't recognize. It said:

> Last night I was watching PBS, and suffering in a
> tremendous amount of pain from endometriosis,
> when your show came on. I loved everything that you
> said, and I felt myself laughing, crying, and relating
> the goddesses to women in my life. Thank you a
> thousand times—your words gave me more relief in
> one hour than doctors have in two painful years!

I read it and wept. That kind of feedback surpassed all my expectations. My heart felt lighter, and my disappointment melted away with the realization that I had genuinely helped someone in need.

Over the next few days, e-mails similar to that one kept coming, random people telling me they'd seen the work while surfing channels and had gotten enjoyment and value from it. The documentary might have been a disappointment in terms of ratings and pledges, but I was beginning to reap its rewards. And this brought with it a liberating lesson: that I had to reframe the concept of "success." The value of the show was immeasurable—the experience of creating it, and now the experience of its touching people—but it could not be measured by the world's standards; all I could do was measure it on my own terms.

It's a funny thing about the word *disappointment*. If you take it apart—*dis-* and *appointment*—it looks as if it could mean something like missing an appointment we've made. Many of the appointments we make are really our expectations: ideas of how things should work out and what success should look like. So often these expectations are unrealistic, based on wishful thinking, and when things don't happen the way we've imagined them, we're left carrying the burden of disappointment.

So expectation/disappointment becomes a vicious cycle, and feeling bad about ourselves and our lives becomes part of everyday life. We go on making and missing the same appointments over and over, creating situations that are bound to let us down, and then we judge ourselves as failures. Each experience in our lives, whether it works out according to our plan or not, is teaching us that we have a choice: to stay open or to close down. Wouldn't it be better if we just entered situations with an attitude of "Let's see how this will turn out," without bringing the pressure of our own agenda to bear?

When we reframe our disappointments in new terms, the way I turned my PBS special into a success of a different kind, we clear the way forward to create new experiences. We need to do this almost daily, just the way we make daily appointments. Then we can give our work a fresh start; we can give a relationship a fresh start; we can create a fresh start in this present moment, right now. We do ourselves a great service when we stop our past from running over into our future.

In Greece, there is a rock on the island of Samos where, legend has it, if you jump off into the Aegean Sea, you'll be cleansed of all your unhappy memories. Just like in the myth of Aphrodite, who every spring went back to her home in Cyprus to bathe in the waters there and renew her virginity—an interesting metaphor for starting each relationship new. I've often thought that if only we could bottle those waters for ourselves, we could renew ourselves every day! But we don't need to leap into the sea to cleanse our hearts of disappointment. All we really need to do is leap into the knowledge that our hearts are so huge they can embrace the little disappointments and transform them into victories.

CHAPTER 14

NO HIDDEN AGENDAS

When I was studying acting in New York, a fellow actress invited me to her house for dinner one night. She had prepared a lovely meal of delicious food and drink, but throughout the dinner, I had a funny feeling in my stomach, as if there was something going on that I couldn't quite pinpoint. If it had been a man putting on this display, I probably would have thought that he was trying to seduce me. With her, however, I couldn't understand the motivation, as we say in the acting world.

At the very end of the evening, we sat down in her living room to have a cup of coffee and chat. It didn't take her long to confess to me that she was pregnant and ask me if I would lend her money for an abortion. I remember my first thought was *I wish she had asked me right up front.* Feeling a little bit on the spot, I told her I would have to think her request over. As it turned out, she called me a few days later to tell me that her boyfriend had agreed to help her. I was relieved not to have to say no *or* yes. But I could only imagine how anxious she must have been during dinner, knowing that dessert would be served up with such a big question.

Very often we encounter situations where we want something from somebody: to advance our career, to advance our social life, perhaps to help someone else we love. We think our connection to them will benefit us in some way, and we may think we can get that benefit without having to come right out and ask. But we are much more transparent than we think. When we want something from others, they usually sense it, and—as with my acquaintance from acting class—it's not only uncomfortable for both parties, it's counterproductive. I have been most successful in getting what I want when I don't try to hide my agenda, if I have one.

I remember when I wanted to produce a TV version of my one-woman show, a good friend of mine invited me to a screening of her own PBS special. When I called her to RSVP, I said to her, "Cathy, I would be very grateful if, at your screening, there is an opportunity to meet the person who runs the station, because I have had an idea for a while to do my one-woman show for PBS. If that doesn't work out, I would love the opportunity to meet her at some other time." She told me that she would be more than happy to make the introduction, and she did. And I trusted that if she hadn't wanted to, she would have told me that just as directly.

This directness was something that my mother taught me—to simply ask people, in a gracious way, for whatever I might want from them. Problems arise when we judge ourselves for what we want from others. We may feel we have no right to ask and don't want to be a bother; we may feel entitled on the one hand or totally undeserving on the other. But this is not true! We do have the right to ask, but we must give the person we are asking the option to respond the way he or she wants to respond—we must keep that door open. When we do this, we are demonstrating our trust that help is available in unlimited supply, if not from that person, then from some other source.

When we act in the belief that this is our only chance or this person is our only connection to what we want, we limit our possibilities—which are otherwise infinite. In my case, if it hadn't been Cathy, it would have been another person. How often do we latch on to something that's in front of us—an interview, a connection, a great date, a career move—and say, "This is it! This is the opportunity that's going to make my dream come true." My mother would always say, "Maybe this is it, and maybe it isn't. Don't limit your solutions."

Hidden agendas show up a lot in personal relationships, and they often block real intimacy. When I lived in New York, I met an adorable Frenchman with whom I had so much fun, going out together and doing interesting things all around the city. He truly cared for me, and I cared for him. Then I started to develop an attraction to him. And whenever we went out in the world together, people always thought we were a couple—which just reinforced my conviction that we could be.

So now I had an agenda: that one day he would discover his attraction for me too. And here's how my agenda played out. Every time we met, I altered myself, projecting an image of what I thought he would like. I stopped being spontaneous and natural—the very things that this man loved about me as a friend. When I think back to what I was doing, it seems kind of insane! Trying to change ourselves so that someone will like us is doomed from the start, because at some point, who we really are is going to be revealed, and if they don't like the real thing now, they never will.

Finally I got fed up with the way I was feeling, and I summoned up the courage to tell him over dinner one night. I remember getting ready to go to that dinner—I must have put on and taken off about ten different tops, as if the top were going to be the deciding factor. As we sat at the table, I found the words I wanted. "I love our friendship, and I enjoy spending time with you. And I am also attracted to you. I would love for us to have more than a friendship, and I want to know if you feel the same way."

Of course, while I was saying it, I was wishing that the earth would open up and swallow me. My stomach was in my throat and the rest of me was in complete and utter disbelief that I was exposing myself in such a way. Still, I wanted so badly for him to want the same. He was so dear and sweet, and I could see in his face that he didn't want to hurt me. He proceeded to tell me he loved me—as a friend. He cared for me and treasured our friendship, but he didn't want to have an intimate relationship.

I don't think I've ever enjoyed dessert as much as I did that night. A weight had lifted from me—hidden agendas are very heavy. My friend walked me to my door, and I exhaled. It did take me a few days to adjust to the reality that there wasn't going to be anything more to that relationship, but the freedom I felt in coming back to myself was worth everything.

CHAPTER 15

A SABBATICAL FROM MEN

It was on a beautiful spring afternoon in New York that a close friend introduced me to someone she thought would be the perfect man for me. He was creative, successful, soulful, sensual, and single, and he was into me!

I had lived in the city before, with my mother and sister, but now, because I was on my own, I felt like it was a different country. Without the haven of my family, I felt very exposed and unprotected. It was as if I were standing in a house in which the floors had not yet been laid.

A part of me was longing to be embraced by a loving, warm man so that I could feel safe and cherished. I thought that the presence of a man in my life was the only way to feel *truly* secure. I deeply desired the intimacy, connection, and joy of a relationship, as well as the solid foundation, and I anticipated that within the stable framework of "us," I could start to lay the planks for my new life.

I believed that this man and I could have all that I had dreamed of. Being with him gave me a lot of the things I was looking for, and we began to build what I thought was real intimacy. He was attentive and interesting, strong and seemingly very present, and the warmth of his presence felt like the family I missed. He loved the arts and theater, as well as music, dance, and food. He had an inner depth that called to me powerfully. In his eyes, I felt accepted and beautiful, free to be myself. I felt that he knew me—really saw me—and that was the greatest aphrodisiac of all. I started to open my heart and take him in.

One night, I called my mother from his apartment, telling her how happy I was. I said, "Mum, I think he is the one!" I wanted him to be the one—for me, for her, and for my whole family, who so wanted me to marry. I was pinning a lot of hopes on this man, expecting him to fill the void in me, the part that felt incomplete and feared to be alone. I was already projecting the happily-ever-after. And, my, was I happy! Was I moving in with him in my mind? Yes. Was I decorating our imaginary home? Yes. All of which is to say that I was going about our relationship too fast, and in the wrong way. I kept looking to him to fill the emptiness. I wanted the experience of being significant to a man, so I could feel valued and whole. My fantasies were headed for a collision with reality. Little did I know that this man was deeply wounded from a childhood with a domineering mother and from a bitter divorce, after which he'd directed all his affections toward his young son. Emotionally, he wasn't available at all.

Six months into our relationship, he had a health scare that required surgery. He told me about it one night as we were lying in bed. He suddenly felt vulnerable, out of control, and very frightened. I, of course, wanted to comfort and nurture him.

He had specifically asked me not to go to the hospital with him, so instead I went to his house the day after, bringing food, games, DVDs, and me. We lay together on his bed eating and talking, and he eventually fell asleep in my arms. My heart was wide open, and the feeling was tender, calm, and sweet. That was the moment when, if words had been spoken, I would have said, "I love you." But something stopped me. It was the fear that if I said it, I would scare him and he would leave me.

What happened after he woke up was a classic example of mismatched expectations. He was anticipating a visit from his family, and I knew it was better for him to be alone with them. So I went back to my apartment, where I waited for him to call and ask me to return and spend the night. Instead, he called and said it was better for him to rest by himself. "Of course," I said. "I understand." But the truth was, I didn't understand. *What went wrong?* I asked myself. *Why doesn't he want me to be with him?*

It took a long time before I realized that I had come up against this man's own closed heart. Perhaps seeing his domineering mother had triggered old fears and hurts. Whatever the reason, when he didn't ask me to come back, I took it personally and felt rejected. If I were to write his script, these are the words he would say to make me understand: *I see your love, I feel your love, but truly, darling, right now there is no place in me to receive it.*

That was the beginning of the end. I had lost my trust in the relationship. I never talked about my feelings; instead, I chose to withdraw. When I saw him again, something had changed. The connection seemed different, and neither of us knew how to restore it.

In this man, I saw my father and other men I had known who were shut down to love. Was it the fear of being controlled? Was it feeling unworthy or undeserving? Or simply the reluctance to risk feeling pain? It takes a lot of courage to make ourselves vulnerable to love, to keep opening up when every part of us wants to shut down. It takes mutual commitment and a willingness to sacrifice our world as we know it. We had reached a point where we were each unwilling to sacrifice and unable to let the other in.

I had to course-correct. I realized that if I wanted to have a healthy, happy relationship with a man, I had to have more of *me* intact. I knew how to merge—that wasn't a problem—but I didn't really know how to stand on my own solid foundation.

The transformation that took place after that realization was quite amazing. I decided I was going to take a sabbatical from men and pull my energy back to me. Whatever part of me believed that I couldn't feel happy and complete without a man's love was going to come under my care and receive my full attention now.

He and I had one more conversation, in which we both admitted that things had shifted, and we agreed to put some distance between us. After that, with no more distractions, no man, my family far away on the West Coast, I had the space to focus on my life by myself. Having been a caretaker all my life, it was a little strange at the beginning: there was no one to take care of but me.

Have you ever seen one of those Advent calendars that children are given before Christmas? Every day you open a little window that has a picture behind it. It can be magical as you wait to see what will come next. That's how I felt—as if I were opening little windows into myself, gaining strength and confidence with each opening. My windows were hiding so many inner riches!

One day I discovered that I could really enjoy being by myself if I had an environment around me that was nurturing and uplifting—so I began to keep my favorite music playing, music that made me happy. Around the same time, I was looking for an assistant to help me with my work, and I realized I needed to choose someone who was joyful and caring and understood my sensibility—so I found a young Argentinean man who made even filing fun. And I found my own rhythm and respected it, so that in the middle of a writing session in my apartment, if my body needed to move, I would take myself out for a walk or a spin class. I learned to listen.

Writing my book became my way to tap those inner riches. Through the goddesses, I was beginning to see my own gifts: my wisdom, my creativity, my love. I realized I had not said no to having a relationship with a man—I had said a big YES to myself, and the windows were popping open.

In one of his dialogues, Plato talks about the "divine design" for each of us—the idea that every person is destined for a task that no one else can accomplish, a path that no one else can take. Writing my first book became, for me, part of that divine design, and it marked the beginning of my new life as a caretaker of my gifts, filling my own cup first so that I could share with others. I copied a quote from Saint Catherine of Siena and kept it on my desk to remind me of the importance of being fully myself: "Be who God meant **you** to be and you will set the world on fire."

CHAPTER 16

TAXI!
TAXI!

Yellow cabs in New York City are like men: you love them, but they don't always love you back when you want them to—especially around 4:30 in the afternoon, because that's when the drivers change shifts, and all of them seem to have their off-duty signs on.

When I lived in New York and was experiencing this particular form of unrequited love, I decided to take matters into my own hands. I was taking a sabbatical from men, but I wasn't taking a sabbatical from taxis. In this particular relationship, I resolved, I was going to be very proactive.

Through all my spiritual practice, I had heard plenty of times that "energy follows thought." I knew all about the power of intention and the secret of the unlimited universe. I also knew that a little of this stuff sometimes goes a long way—but I did love the idea that if you want something, you should simply hold the thought of it steadily in your mind and not focus on your lack of it. I decided to test the theory by making yellow cabs appear.

I practiced by standing on a busy corner with my hand in the air, directing all my attention to the idea of a yellow cab. On a crowded stretch of Seventh Avenue at 4:30 in the afternoon, I would stand there and really focus, holding the intention that a taxi would show up. Imagining that I could connect telepathically with the taxi fleet, I would think, *Now, come on, there has got to be one of you free in all of New York City at this moment—and why not be free in front of me?* And you know what? It started working. Sometimes a taxi would pull up right in front of me to let another passenger out, and I'd pop in. Sometimes one would come by with its *Off Duty* sign on, but I'd flag it down anyway, and the driver would say, "I'm going your way. Hop in." In extreme situations, I might spot someone else getting into a taxi and ask the person if we could share, at which point they would usually give me a look—*Who is this odd woman who wants to get into my taxi?* But once in a while, I got a ride that way.

I used all sorts of methodologies to get the desired outcome: a taxi. I experimented until I became a taxi magnet. I started to have fun with this game! I remember one night when I was on a date. We had just left the restaurant and were heading to the theater, and my date said, "This is a terrible corner—we're never going to get a taxi here! We should walk a few blocks to where it's less crowded."

"Don't worry," I said, "we can get one here." Then I asked him to go across the street because his belief was going to interfere with mine. He looked at me a bit uncertainly, but he complied. Sure enough, a few minutes later a taxi pulled up right in front of me, two people got out, my date rushed over, and we hopped in. My date asked me, "How did you do that?" And I replied, "I have been practicing." My taxi magnet was working.

I started to realize that I could apply this same methodology in other significant areas of my life. I just had to approach them with the same focus I brought to my taxi practice. I would need to state my intention in a spirit of unlimited possibility. It was important not to put any doubt or limiting beliefs between me and what I wanted to happen. For example, years later, when I wanted to turn my one-woman show into a PBS special, I wrote this phrase in my organizer: *PBS special—completed successfully.* Then I put a check mark next to it. I got a very clear picture of the end result, even though I hadn't the faintest idea how I was going to bring it about. I just held that picture in my mind. The taxi was a symbol for me, showing me that I wasn't alone in this world in creating what I wanted to create—that help was always available, if I cared to ask for it. That gave me tremendous confidence and inner security whenever I felt stuck. It awakened a sense of magic in my life.

I became so passionate about the success of this technique that I actually started giving seminars on it, called "Discovering Your Golden Opportunities." I gave each participant a little yellow cab along with the course materials, because that had been my first experiment, in which I learned how I could achieve the results I wanted. What I realized, and shared with the course participants, was that by acknowledging the things we have already accomplished in our lives, we affirm our strengths and transfer those strengths to the things that are challenging for us. Becoming conscious of the conversation that's going on inside our heads gives us the chance to choose what voice we are going to listen to.

In one of my seminars there was a divorced woman in her late 50s who believed that love would never come her way again. The conversation in her head went something like this: *I am too old . . . there are no men around . . . and if there are, they only want 30-year-olds . . .* and on and on. I told her that could very well be true for some men, but if there was one man somewhere on the planet who was *her* man, looking for her, that was all she really needed: one. I encouraged her to consciously choose different thoughts so she could see the new possibilities in her life. Could she somehow shift her focus? Paradigm shifts start small, but with focus and discipline, they gain momentum to get you where you want to go. Imagine if I had sat on the curb on Seventh Avenue, letting my negative thoughts play in a constant loop: *It's always so hard to get a taxi . . . this is the worst time of day . . . there are no taxis anywhere . . .* I probably wouldn't have noticed a taxi if it passed right under my nose! Thoughts like these become self-fulfilling prophecies.

When I ran into friends who had taken my seminar, I was delighted to hear that so many of the things they wanted were coming through. Sometimes I would get voice mails from people saying, "You're not going to believe what I made happen today!" Once, when I needed to make a recording of a guided meditation for a workshop I was conducting, I was on a shoestring budget and looking for a studio I could afford. I had asked a few friends if they could help me. One day one of them called me, saying, "I have just found you a $3,000-a-day studio in Burbank—for free!" It's another example of how effective asking for help in a spirit of openness can be.

I have discovered that helping others in getting what they want is a shortcut to realizing this ability in ourselves, because when we are serving someone else, we get out of our own way and we can see the possibilities much more clearly. When people come to us and ask for our help in opening some door—whether they're looking for a house within their budget, or a connection that might lead to a job, or a good school for their kids—I realize that each one of us can be our own Make-a-Wish Foundation and make someone else's wish come true. So many people have been there for me to realize my dreams, and when I can be there for others to help them do the same, I become part of the circle of giving and receiving that makes life so rich.

The other day, I was driving to an event with a friend, and when we got to the gate, there was a sign in the driveway that said: *LOT IS FULL*. I looked at my friend and said, "Maybe yes, maybe no," and I drove in anyway. And on our first circuit around the parking lot, sure enough, we found an empty spot at the very end of a row. My taxi magnet was working! Even when it looks like there are no taxis anywhere in sight, or no spaces in the parking lot—or whatever we think is missing in our lives—our beliefs are more powerful than any man-made signs, and there is always space for us, if we choose to claim it.

CHAPTER 17

ME, MEN, AND MY MOTHER

Tom Stoppard's play *The Real Thing* contains a monologue in which the central character, Henry, talks to his daughter about love and betrayal. Having just learned of his actress wife's affair with her leading man, he speaks about the real thing that two lovers hold between them: "It's what lovers trust each other with. Knowledge of each other, not of the flesh but through the flesh, knowledge of self, the real him, the real her, *in extremis,* the mask slipped from the face." Henry says that that knowledge is "the undealt card, and while it's held it makes you free-and-easy and nice to know, and when it's gone everything is pain. Every single thing." There is nothing left, because something essential has been betrayed.

I always loved that monologue because of what it conveys. I understand the real thing, the part of ourselves that—beyond all the daily whirl, all the talking and connecting, all the engagements and obligations to the world and even to our closest friends—we choose to share with just one other or keep to ourselves. Mostly, it's the part that we share with our spouse or a lover in an intimate relationship, which stays contained until we are willing to share it.

I remember some time ago I came across a picture of my mother pushing a pram with my sister and me inside it. I was just a baby, asleep, while my older sister was sitting up in the pram, holding her doll. My mother's face in the photograph was beautiful, yet it was shadowed by a veil of sorrow. I now know that it was because my father had started having affairs. The real thing, that sacred knowledge that they had shared, had been betrayed. I believe that emotions can be transferred through our unconscious, without words, from our parents to us. I think that even at that point I was already absorbing my mother's fear and her broken faith in relationships, which only became more pronounced as I grew older and witnessed my parents' unhappiness and difficult marriage. I could feel my mother's pain and her unspoken fears for me. A voice in me was saying, *I don't want this ever to happen to me,* and I think that voice was coming from her, saying, *I don't want this ever to happen to you.*

For a long time I took it upon myself to heal my father's wounded heart, thinking that if I were there with him wholeheartedly, he would be able to love my mother back. Then I would be released from my sense of having to watch over her, free to live my life. It was so liberating when finally, as an adult, I became fully aware that it was not my responsibility to heal either of them. I could simply love them.

As I got on with my life, I had many types of relationships. I fell in love with a man but the love wasn't returned; a man fell in love with me but I didn't love him back; we both fell in love but then fell out of it. I played out every possible configuration, and always with the thought lurking that there was one person who was my perfect match.

People were always surprised that I, a passionate Greek woman with nurturing in her blood, wasn't married with a house full of kids. My father used to joke, "We've sent you all over the world. Why can't you find one man to marry?" I would joke right back, "Maybe you should just have sent me to a Greek village—then I'd definitely be married, to my next-door neighbor!"

In later years, I had a very powerful experience with love. There was a man whom I fell madly in love with and who loved me back. We had moments of the "real thing," and he transported me from Planet Earth to Venus for a while. But when we tried to make it work on Planet Earth, gravity got in the way. However, I became addicted to whatever potion is released from that strong mutual attraction. Extricating myself from that relationship and coming out of it intact took every ounce of will I had and an exhaustive number of prayers. I grew stronger from it, wiser, and more compassionate when other people came to me with similar experiences. Then I could say to them, "I know the hurt, and I know the pain, but I also know the freedom once you are on the other side of it."

When I reflected on my past relationships, a pattern emerged of emotional unavailability, often on both our parts. To heal, I needed to distinguish between my mother's beliefs that I had internalized and those that were truly mine. I was not my mother. I had to accept that her feelings about my father, her hurt and betrayal, and her disappointment in men, were hers to bear; then I could allow myself the freedom to have my own experiences, not prejudging but trusting my own discernment and wisdom. There's a wonderful feeling of release—almost like exhaling—when we start to follow our own compass instead of one that we've inherited.

Some years later, when I was living in Santa Barbara, I was asked to act in a play called *Love Letters* by A. R. Gurney, which consists of one man and one woman on a stage, reading aloud their letters to each other, which span five decades. The play has been performed by many different actors and actresses over the years, some of them real couples. A friend suggested that I contact the man I had fallen in love with when I first moved to Los Angeles—remember the actor with the macrobiotic breakfasts?—and ask him to do the play with me.

I hadn't spoken to this man in years. I called him to ask if he wanted to act in the play with me. He was pleasantly surprised to hear from me. As we were catching up, he told me that he was married and had two sons, but that he was going through a hard time in his marriage. My calling him was timely, he said, because he needed to do something creative. When he asked about me, I told him that I wasn't married. Immediately, he responded, "But that was never your dream."

It hit me like a lightning bolt how right he was. At the same time, I was astounded that he had that much insight into me. I had never admitted, even to myself, that that was not my dream.

What was my dream, then? My dream was to find my creative expression and realize it to its fullest extent and to be totally used up by life, by God. If a man wandered in while I was in the middle of doing this, and he could be part of that dream, he was welcome, but I wasn't going out of my way to make it happen.

I was talking to my spiritual teacher around my birthday one year, and I found myself sharing my feelings about another year spent alone. "I'm still single," I said wistfully, as if something were missing. And in his wonderful, soulful, matter-of-fact way, he looked at me and said, "You're singular." In that moment, he took away any negative charge that the idea of being single still held for me. I so loved this new perspective of being singular. *Singular* gave me a sense of wholeness and freedom, with unlimited possibility—not bound by fears or longings, but open to sharing the abundance of love in whatever form it took. Now, if I choose an intimate relationship, I see it as a partnership, arising not out of need or lack, but out of the happiness of sharing life and who we are—the real thing.

CHAPTER 18

NO MORE LONGING

One summer, I was eating out with some friends in New York and found myself sitting next to a wonderful, exuberant woman who was visiting from Florida. We very quickly got to talking about the things that matter. She told me that she was divorced, with adult children, and was running her own business in Florida. She had been an avid ballroom dancer for several years, and she adored her teacher, with whom she danced in competitions and other events. She was lively and confident, and on the surface, she seemed to have a charmed life.

As it happened, I was going salsa dancing at Lincoln Center that Friday. It would be at one of the events they hold there in the summer, where couples dance to live bands that play beside the fountain in the plaza. I was planning to go on my own and meet some friends there, and I invited my new friend to come along.

"Oh, I don't think so," she said.

"But you love to dance!"

"I just can't," she said sadly. Then she confessed to me that she couldn't go dancing alone because it hurt too much to see all those happy couples in each other's arms. It broke her heart that she didn't have a dancing partner with whom she could also share her life.

I was astounded. It had never occurred to me to avoid dancing because I didn't have a partner. In the exuberant Greek way of life I was brought up in, you could pull anyone onto the dance floor, and he or she would be your partner for the night. Not having a partner never stopped me from dancing.

When the dinner party broke up, my new friend and I walked down Sixth Avenue together, talking about why she didn't have a partner and what she was looking for in one. She said to me, "I've been longing for the right person for years now, ever since I was divorced. Someone I'm compatible with and can have fun with. Someone I can enjoy my life with and also dance with. I get very upset when I think that other people have that and I don't. I wonder, 'Why not me?'"

This wanting-and-not-having is part of the human condition, I reflected. *We all want something we can't get. But when the not-having causes us pain, it can cause us to withdraw from loving and close ourselves down.*

"Is it not okay to want a man?" she went on. "Or a relationship?"

"Of course it's okay," I said. "But there's a difference between wanting and longing." *Longing* is about attachment, I explained, and attachment creates suffering. It grabs on to things with long, long tentacles, and it suffocates our enjoyment of life. *Wanting* is about information and opportunity. If you get clear about what you want and why, then you can go about finding ways to create it. "I used to long for an ideal partner too," I told my new friend. "But when I gave up the longing, I started to enjoy my life much more. The longing was just creating unhappiness for me. What if you gave up your longing and started thinking about how to make it a reality instead?"

"I don't want to give up my longing!" she exclaimed. "It reminds me of how much I want a partner, and I don't want to forget that."

"That's okay," I replied, "provided that your longing doesn't keep you from being present."

She stopped in her tracks, right in the middle of Sixth Avenue, and took my hand. "Wait," she said. "I'm having an epiphany. Don't say anything else." After a few moments, she looked at me with a new expression. She said, "I never realized that my longing was preventing me from being present." She was internalizing this shift in perspective, seeing how longing perpetuates desire and how that just keeps us in a state of not getting what we want. We continued on down the avenue, and thanks to that epiphany, we were both walking a little taller.

It seems as if the world hardwires us for longing. Our society has put it on a pedestal, in literature, movies, television, and song. Elizabeth Bennet longs for Mr. Darcy, Scarlett O'Hara longs for Rhett Butler, Carrie Bradshaw longs for Mr. Big, the shadowy Phantom of the Opera sings his heart out for Christine.

But it's not just romantic love we long for. We long for financial success, we long for the perfect career. We long for a better body, a beach vacation, an adventure in a faraway land. We long to write that book or get that part. We long for recognition, we long for the opportunities we see other people getting. And many people long for connection with God. My friend had it right: our longing can come between us and the object of our desire. It can be a defense mechanism, keeping us from risking disappointment if we try and fail. But it's when we let go of longing that our dreams really come within reach.

Naturally, not everyone is going to have an epiphany in the middle of the street like my friend. If you don't happen to experience one yourself, simply focus on what it is you desire, and then strip away the longing. Take what's left and distill it—the essence of your desire fulfilled. Look at my friend, who wanted a partner she could dance with: for her, the bottom-line experience was *having a connection to someone I love who loves me back*. Now think about what it feels like to have what you desire—the sense of aliveness and empowerment it brings, the way it fills your heart. Bring that feeling alive in all your senses. Touch it, hear it, see it, feel it in your entire body, until *you* embody it.

On your path toward your desired outcome, you may come across obstacles you've put there yourself. So often, we block our own way with judgments and conditions. We decide we can't have what we want, we worry because we aren't getting what we want, we're afraid of what will happen if we never get it—and sometimes afraid of what will happen if we do. We often get a glimpse of what we want our life to be, but doubt can cloud our vision and stop us from trying before we even start. Don't give in to those thoughts—assert your authority over them. Remember, they're only real if you pay attention to them.

We think that in order to get where we want to go, we need to know every step of the way. In truth, we don't. Sometimes it's as simple as putting one foot in front of the other, holding the vision of where we're going, and trusting that the path will take us there. I think of what the celebrated writer E. L. Doctorow once said about the act of writing: "It's like driving a car at night. You never see further than your headlights, but you can make the whole trip that way."

CHAPTER 19

YOUR PORTABLE PARADISE

There was a game I used to play when I was four years old, with one of my favorite sitters, an older girl, around 15. I would hide someplace and I would ask her if God could see me there. I'd hide under the table, under the bed, in the closet, behind a tree in the garden, and I'd ask her, "Can God see me here? What about here? Can he see me here?" as I ran from hiding place to hiding place with all the innocence of that precious age.

And my sitter would say, "Yes, God can see you everywhere. This is because he is everywhere. You can't hide from him."

I don't know how this topic came up when I was four, or what put the question in my mind. But it made perfect sense to me then that the presence of God was everywhere. It wasn't until later that I lost touch with that essential truth.

As we grow up, it's as if a veil drops between us and the pure, essential awareness with which we came into the world. We begin our education, we adapt to our environment, and we conform to the ways of our family, community, and society; gradually, all these things put layers between us and the presence of God, or Spirit, or whatever name we choose to give it. We develop the drive to achieve—we earn degrees, we go after success, we enter relationships, we build a life for ourselves—and the hurts and disappointments that come from living can start to affect us. We develop an idea of who and what we are supposed to become that moves us away from simply being who we are. And as we step more and more fully into this worldly identity, we can get hooked into it, at the expense of our soul.

That's what happened to me. At a tender age, I was all innocence and openness; love was what I was all about. Then, as I grew into my teenage years, a deep desire to become a star took hold of me. I think it was born out of the hurt of my parents' separation, which left me feeling unsure of my place. I had formed the belief that I wasn't lovable unless I was recognized by the world. On my to-do list, there was "Study for math test" and "Make birthday card for Daddy" and "Go to dance class," and at the bottom was always "Be famous," lest I forget. As time went on, I got more and more convinced that I had to become a star in order to be seen and known—that my very existence depended on it. I got so hooked into the worldly identity I'd fashioned for myself that if God himself had come and sat at my feet and said, "I am here," I would have replied, "I can't see you right now.

I am too busy becoming somebody. I'll have to get back to you."

It was only later in my life, when I had forgotten what I knew so well when I was four years old—and when the fame thing wasn't happening—that I would want to see God as much as the four-year-old wanted to *be* seen and the 14-year-old wanted to be famous. That's when I started to knock on doors, giving my spiritual search my whole mind, body, and soul. I wanted to lift that veil as much as I wanted my next breath. And I wanted to be happy. I didn't like the pain I was in; I didn't think it fit my nature. I was determined to get free.

We crave connection to Spirit, but our society doesn't exactly support us in this quest. There are plenty of signposts along our path directing us to work hard, look good, make money, get married, and on and on, but there are no signs reminding us to stay connected to the essence of who we are. We see placards that say, *Please remember to take your personal belongings*, but there are none to tell us, *Please be sure not to leave your soul behind.* You don't get an Oscar for keeping an open heart, and you'll never see a résumé with the bullet point "Have preserved my original innocence." Can you imagine? You'd never get in the door for the interview!

I believe that no matter how hooked on our worldly personas we get, deep down in our human hearts we're still asking that same four-year-old's question: *Can I be seen here? Can God see me here?* But we're so focused on looking for the answer outside ourselves—thinking that God is "out there" somewhere—that we forget to look inward. Instead, we look to the next book, teacher, seminar, or religious service to give us back what we think we're missing, that original connection we were born with. Sometimes we imagine that we can regain it through other people—our families, children, spouses, lovers, and friends. We fall in love and we think that will do it, and sometimes it does for a bit. Then we fall out of love and we're back in the search again. And there's nothing wrong with seeking connection in this way, but it's not a substitute for the direct connection that is available for us—yes, just for us, exactly as we are!

We know the truth when we are four years old: when we ask, "Can God see me here?" the answer is always yes. The warm and loving presence of Spirit is everywhere. There is no place we can go where that presence is not; no place we can hide. We don't need to prove ourselves or manipulate our circumstances in any way in order to regain that essential connection. What we can do, however, what we need to do, is peel away the layers and come back to the truth we've always known, that Spirit never leaves our lives. The wonderful thing about veils is that they are there to be lifted.

Several years ago a dear friend of mine was going through what you might call a midlife crisis. She had immersed herself in creating her own business, and as the business had gotten more and more successful, she had fallen more and more out of touch with herself. The concern for the bottom line, the need to compete, and the stress of trying to survive an economic meltdown had taken over her life completely. She had become her business.

During that time, my friend and her family took a trip to Greece for her mother's 80th birthday. They stayed on the island of Santorini, where the sunsets over the volcanic caldera are among the most glorious in the world, and the sea air, the fresh food, and the warmth of the people all reconnect you with the essential joy of life. As wrapped up in her business as my friend was, she felt herself starting to relax as she and her family celebrated her mother's life and toasted her with the luscious Santorini wine. Early one morning, she went for a run on the beach, and suddenly she realized that she felt more alive than she had in years.

Her mother's birthday party had been a joyous celebration. Running along the red sand as the sun was rising out of the sea, my friend remembered her mother's face lit up with pleasure—and as she pictured that aging face, she realized she had been working all her life not to be like her mother, who had had a bad marriage and a dysfunctional family and always struggled to make ends meet. My friend was the only one of her siblings to really "make it," and she saw in a flash that the real motivation behind all her hard work had been to prove herself—to make sure that she wouldn't turn out like the rest of them. She understood that she had been going about it the wrong way—focusing on what she did not want to be, instead of working to bring her true gifts to the world—and that *that* was the greatest stress of all.

The clarity of this awareness was startling, and she wanted to hold on to it. She didn't want to lose the new sense of aliveness and connection that she felt in this beautiful place. *I don't want to leave here,* she thought—and so, as she ran, she started to daydream about staying. Lots of people did business from remote locations. What would it be like to live and work in this paradise of sun and sea?

In her hotel room, some lines from the 20th-century poet Constantine Cavafy were stenciled on the wall, a common decorative feature in Greek hotels. When my friend got back to her room after her run, the lines from Cavafy's poem "The City" caught her eye, and she read them with new attention: *You said, "I'll go to another country, to another shore, / find another city better than this one. . . ."*

But the poem goes on to say that there is no way to get to that new land—that wherever you go, you bring your old life with you. And it dawned on my friend, like the real dawn, that she wasn't going to move her whole family to Santorini. She wasn't going to relocate her business to a Greek island. That just wasn't feasible! What she *could* do was take the feeling she had found there and integrate it into her real life at home. She could carry the spirit of Santorini home with her.

Spirit meets us where we are, in any place and in any moment. It doesn't come to us only when everything is clean, organized, and perfect in our world. Spirit doesn't stand on ceremony. You can have a beautiful table set with napkins that match the tablecloth, or you can have a picnic spread out under an olive tree—Spirit will join you either way. My mother said that some of her most spiritual experiences were washing dishes or feeding the seagulls at the beach. It doesn't come only when we get promotions or awards; it is there when we get fired, when we lose our homes, when we get sick, when we get left behind. And if we experience it as absent, then it's because we've turned away from it ourselves.

Countless things happen in the course of a day that seem to pull us away. And yet Spirit rises up in me even when I'm waiting for my luggage at the airport, tired and irritable, and a nice young man helps me pick up my heavy bags, or when I'm in line at the supermarket and I give my place to someone who's standing impatiently behind me. I make it a habit to call upon Spirit a hundred times a day, dressed or undressed, ten pounds lighter or heavier, in an important meeting, in the quiet of my garden, or in a traffic jam on the freeway. The amazing thing I've found is that when my awareness of that connection starts to slip, all it takes is a small shift to bring it back into focus. Spirit is as close as our next breath.

When my friend got home from her trip to Santorini, she called the whole company together for a meeting so that all her employees could voice how they felt about their jobs. Then she started planning ways to bring a greater sense of community and connection into their work. She renovated the offices in a new spirit of beauty and openness, and one of the first things she did was take down the cubicle walls to create a big open workspace, where people could see one another and light could pour in.

In her own office, my friend keeps pictures of the Greek seacoast—the sun and skies, the blues and turquoises of the Aegean. She says that a glimpse of that bright horizon can instantly bring her back to the connection she felt there. Some people trek across Antarctica to find that connection, and some climb up the Himalayas. Other people meet Spirit in near-death experiences, coming back with a memory of the other side. But we don't have to almost die to find it. We don't have to go to the ends of the earth, and we don't have to "get there"—anywhere—in order to restore the connection. It's ours for the claiming.

Then, with the innocence of a four-year-old, we can turn back to what has been right there all along: the assurance of God's presence in our own personal, portable paradise.

CHAPTER 20

CHANGE THE
CHANNEL

For several years, I tried to produce a film on the life story of Maria Callas, based on a book my sister had written. Callas was a Greek opera singer who became one of the most celebrated sopranos in the world. She then fell in love with the shipping magnate Aristotle Onassis, who broke her heart when he left her for Jacqueline Kennedy. It's the story of a woman who allowed herself to be overpowered by a man who had no idea how to honor, cherish, and truly value her—and she had no idea how to value herself beyond her enormous artistic achievements. Her sense of lovability was dependent on this man's love. What had always intrigued me about her story, and what I wanted to bring to the screen, was how somebody so brilliant in one area of life could be so paralyzed in another.

I had a Greek business partner who loved the project as much as I did and had invested money in its development. A well-known actress showed interest, and she brought in a very well-known Italian director who had known and worked with Maria. We hired him, for a substantial retainer, to develop the script with the writer of his choice. There were contracts, meetings, first-class tickets from Rome to L.A., my mother's Greek dinners, lots of enthusiasm and excitement over what could have been a dream come true. But nine months later, we had nothing to show for it but a letter stating that the Italian director wanted to write the script himself and keep all the rights to the movie, effectively cutting us out. It's the classic Hollywood story of "Screw you!"

I was hurt and angry, and I felt like a victim because I couldn't take any action. My lawyer said we couldn't sue the director because he lived in another country, so we might as well kiss the project goodbye. I walked away completely discouraged, blaming myself, filled with disappointment, unable to put closure to it. Everyone around me sympathized and told me I had a right to feel I had been wronged. My Greek partner was fuming as well, and that wasn't making it any better.

My mother, however, knew when it was time to move on. Over dinner one night, as I was replaying the story for the hundredth time—*should have, could have, if only I had*—she decided to help me break the pattern. "Darling," she said, "change the channel." That was her famous expression, used whenever someone seemed anxious, fearful, agitated, or blue for too long.

"What should I change it to?" I asked.

"Anything," she said. "The Golf Channel! You've been switching between the Disappointment Channel and the Blame Yourself Channel for too long."

To her, the point was that we didn't have to be at the mercy of our habitual emotional thinking: we were the ones holding the clicker. So I decided to change the channel! I still had the rights to my sister's book, and I could move on. So took the project to a studio and started all over again, with newfound enthusiasm—and more detachment this time.

We all have habitual patterns of negative thinking, feeling, and doing that sabotage our happiness. They become so ingrained that we think we have no power to change them. They simply become part of our daily life, and they start to constrict us.

Are you familiar with the Greek myth of Sisyphus? A crafty and arrogant man, he was condemned by Zeus for his evil deeds to roll a rock up a hill, only to have it roll right back down just before he could get it to the top. He would have to repeat this task day after day for eternity. So every day he rolled that rock up the hill, and lo and behold, down it came again. Talk about being stuck on one channel!

Sisyphus was under a spell. All of us, in one way or another, put our own unconscious spells on ourselves. What could he do to shake it off? He could shout for help—two people rolling the rock is easier than one. Or he could push a little bit harder—maybe that last push would be all it took to get the rock to the top and down the other side. But I think my mother would have said to him, "Sisyphus, darling, change the channel!"

Imagine what would have happened if Sisyphus woke up one morning and said, "This is a myth! I don't have to push that rock up and down ever again if I don't want to." Then he might have sat down on the rock and admired the view of the mountain. Or decided to look at the rock-pushing as a pleasant pastime. Or moved to a place where there were no rocks or mountains at all. What if Sisyphus knew that he had the choice to change the story?

The point is that we are much more in charge than we think. We're the ones who are holding the remote control. I was able to change the channel when I got the lesson—and the lesson was that, because I had been seduced by the talent and fame of this man, I had ignored the red flags that were all over the place from the beginning. I was so impressed with the fact that this celebrated Italian director wanted to direct the movie I so loved that I let him call the shots. I didn't read between the lines (or between the dinners, the lunches, and the power meetings) to see what the intention really was— never an intention to make this movie, apparently. I knew from my mother not to be seduced by the power of money or fame—but talent was another matter. In the presence of a great talent that I admired, I was seduced, and it shook me deeply.

I believe we bring these challenging experiences on ourselves so that we can discover the patterns that bind us. What are the belief systems we're living by that undermine who we are? When we shed enough light on them, we liberate ourselves, and then we can easily change the channel. The profound awareness I came to was that no matter how much more experienced the other person was, I didn't have to put my own discernment on hold or give my authority over. I could stay centered in myself and enjoy the gifts that others brought to the table without diminishing my own.

CHAPTER 21

A HANDFUL
OF NAILS

In Greece, human warmth and connection are written into the cultural code. People reach out to each other. They chat on the street whether they know each other or not. Men whistle at women as they walk by, and it's taken as a compliment—a boost for the female ego! Not knowing your neighbors is unthinkable. And when you ask people how they are, they tell you what they feel in the moment, whether happy or discouraged, ecstatic or upset. They know that uncensored expression is good for the soul.

People often return home from trips to Greece with stories that illustrate the famous Greek hospitality. One friend met a woman on a village street who spontaneously invited her into her home and baked her cookies. A market vendor gave another friend the hand-woven shawl she was admiring—for free. In these acts of un-bounded generosity, there are no hidden agendas such as *I'll do this for you; now what are you going to do for me?* People extend themselves simply for the sake of doing it. Why? Because our heart is fed by this unconditional act. Every other part of us grows by receiving—our body, our emotions, and our minds—but our heart grows by giving.

The deeper you go into the Greek countryside, the more you find this warmth of hearth and heart. This unconditional way of being, this need for connecting, breaks the iciness of isolation and the illusion that we are separate. People provide for each other, even for their most basic needs, and it is contagious. The community is one extended family, and if you spend a little time in a place like this, you become part of that family, too.

After my sister published her book on the Greek gods, she was asked to do a feature for *Town & Country* in which she was photographed in Greece, dressed as each of the gods and goddesses. For her photo as Diony-sus, god of wine, we drove to a friend's vineyard outside Athens and gathered on the porch of the little house where the caretaker, Mr. Vasilios, lived with his wife and daughter. He welcomed us with typical Greek hospital-ity, offering ouzo, feta cheese, olives, grapes, and bread. The photographer wanted to hang bunches of grapes from the porch beams to take a shot of my sister's face surrounded by the fruit. We asked Mr. Vasilios if he had a few nails we could pound into the beams.

Mr. Vasilios put his hand on his head, pondering out loud, "Nails, nails, nails," as if he were going to manifest them from thin air. Suddenly his gaze fell on a three-legged stool in the porch's far corner. "Ah, nails," he exclaimed—and proceeded to pull out the nails that held the stool together. He handed them to us with a look of triumph. "Here are six nails!" We glanced at each other, speechless. Such generosity—taking apart the furniture to loan strangers a few nails—is what I call uncondi-tional giving, being so open to someone else's needs that you will go to any length to meet them. Each time we do this from the heart, life becomes richer, more full of meaning.

Unconditional giving is possible anywhere and at any time. I once saw a billboard with a picture of Mother Teresa and the words "Compassion. Reach out beyond yourself." But reaching out in generosity doesn't have to be on the scale of a saint, nor does it need to have a label like "feeding the homeless" or "saving the children." A small, simple gesture also has the power to connect us. My mother's life was filled with such moments. Wher-ever she was—in an elevator, a taxi, an airplane, a park-ing lot, the supermarket, the bank—she would reach out to others in an open-hearted way. Once, a stranger admired the necklace she was wearing, and my mother took it off and gave it to her. When the astonished wom-an asked, "What can I give you in return?" my mother said, "It's not a trade, darling, it's an offering."

When she went to the doctor, she always arrived with a bottle of wine or a basket of fruit for the nurses. She knew that in an office where patients brought their wor-ries and pains, the gesture would change the atmosphere. Her tenacity in breaking through the barriers that people put up around their hearts was both magical and comical. If one of the nurses was, as she put it, "on automatic" and didn't take the time to be friendly or personal, my mother would whisper to me, "This one doesn't want to budge," and would start looking for a way to give her extra attention. She might produce a little treat from her purse—a package of nuts, a special kind of chocolate—and give it to the woman, knowing she would get a smile. This practice gave her tremendous joy.

The rest of us might protest, "I could never do that. I'd feel so awkward. I might get rejected, and then I'd feel worse." That's the wrong way of looking at it, because it's not about us. The giving is for other people's sake, and we get to partake in the experience.

One thing I learned in acting was that if you want to get into the character you're playing, you have to get out of your own way. The very first time I performed the one-woman show I'd conceived and written, there was a strange timidity in me; I was entering unknown territory. Then I heard the voice of my acting teacher saying, *Don't think about yourself—think about what you have to say to the audience and how much you want to say it. Think about them, not you.* After that, I never again felt nervous or anxious before going onstage—just excited about how wonderful it was to share my passion. I was bursting at the seams with excitement!

That's the great secret: when we give unconditionally, our own hearts are filled. If you want to know the true power of your heart, make something good happen for someone else. When we do that, we discover the hidden abundance that is all around us, and we discover a handful of nails where we thought there were none.

CHAPTER 22

THE ELEPHANT IN THE ROOM

When my first book came out, I had lunch with the publicist to talk about the book's promotion. I was full of enthusiasm, bubbling over with ideas about product tie-ins and speaking engagements—but as I went on, I felt that I was talking to a blank wall. Nothing was coming back to me: no feedback, no responses, no energy at all. The woman just sat there staring blankly at me, nodding once in a while.

Finally I had to ask, "Is everything all right with you?"

Her eyes filled with tears. "I'm sorry," she said, "I'm very preoccupied." And she told me that her ex-husband had committed suicide four days earlier. "I don't know how to deal with it," she went on. "We weren't close anymore, but I'm worried about our daughter." Then she apologized again and tried to bring the discussion back to my book.

"My goodness," I said, "this is much more important to talk about than book promotion!" And we proceeded to have an honest, deep conversation—which would never have happened if I had gone on ignoring her obvious discomfort. I call an issue like this the elephant in the room. It was something huge, right there at the table with us, and I just could not pretend that it wasn't there.

Her ex-husband's suicide had come as a terrible shock to her, because she had thought he was happily remarried; she didn't know he had such hidden pain. So many of us have pain in our hearts that we don't want to reveal—sometimes not even to ourselves. We fear that if we face the pain and allow ourselves to feel it, we'll get stuck and never come out of it. It's safer just to pretend that the pain isn't there. So we go on in our daily lives, not sharing it with anyone, living in disguise, and doing a great disservice to ourselves.

So many times in my own life, when I've felt hurt, upset, or insecure, it has seemed easier to hide that hurt by stuffing it down and covering it up, sweeping it under the rug and trying to forget about it. But pain that's hidden like that can wind up being the elephant in the room, and that elephant is *big!* You can cover the elephant with blankets, put a pretty bow on him, or try to disguise him as a sofa, but he is still there. When people come to visit, you can squeeze him into the corner and try to act like there is no elephant around, but he is there all the same. In fact, his trunk is so long that he can reach out from under the blankets and pick you up and twirl you around until you don't know which way is up.

And then you're in a heap on the floor and he's taking up the whole room!

In wartime, "seeing the elephant" is a slang phrase that soldiers use to describe going into combat for the first time. After that, there is no longer the formless fear of something they can't face. They know the reality and they know they can face it, because they have already done so. I think it's the same with that old elephant in your living room. When you're trying your hardest *not* to see him, the glimpses you get from the corner of your eye just make him loom larger. The only way to take his true measure is to face him straight on. That's when you notice that you are actually much bigger than the elephant after all. Then you can tie a rope around his trunk and lead him gently out of the living room. At some point, you can lead him all the way out of the house, and there you can let him go.

So how do we face the things that we think we can't face? We have to turn toward our pain and go straight into it, because the only way out is through. We don't need to worry that we'll get stuck in the hurting places, as long we look directly at what we see there and call it by its name. Sorrow at losing love, the hurt of being betrayed or shunned, the pain of being unable to help a loved one, dissatisfaction at work, shame for being over-weight, guilt for hurting a friend, knowing we've betrayed ourselves by compromising our truth. When we are honest with ourselves and speak truthfully what is hidden in that closed, secret place, we dislodge the pain that has been keeping our hearts bound.

In Greece, when you ask people how they are, the answer is never, "I'm fine." No one is ever "fine." They take the time to be specific about their emotional states, so they usually respond with "I'm happy" or "I'm worried" or "I'm tired today" or "I am furious!" It's very freeing to name what you're feeling. Stating where you are sends a very strong message that you have a right to your feelings—and it gives you the choice to transform them. If you're unhappy but you suppress it by saying, "I'm fine," you have nowhere to go. But if you say, "I'm unhappy," you can explore the things that are making you feel that way, and then you can work toward happiness. When you name your feelings to yourself, you're back in charge, and you feel more authentic, connected to yourself and other people.

Imagine that a friend comes to visit you when you are dealing with something that's troubling you. It takes a huge amount of energy to pretend there's no elephant in the room—so imagine you don't even try! You just say, "Oh, by the way, this is my elephant." Can you imagine how liberating that would be?

"That's funny," your guest may say. "I have an elephant just like that one. I haven't decided what to do with him."

"I already shrunk mine," you say, "and I'm thinking of letting him go pretty soon." And once you've gotten that out of the way, you can start to talk about the things that really matter.

Not long ago, I had dinner with a friend and her father, who was visiting from out of town. A dynamic, successful neuroscientist, he had been widely recognized for his innovative thinking and achievements. My friend, by contrast, was a talented artist who did beautiful, expressive work but had yet to receive much recognition in the world. It was clear that her father loved her very much, but he talked mostly about his own life and work, and the impression I got was of a man who was rather full of himself. During dinner, I sensed that my friend was unusually withdrawn, not as engaged or energetic as I knew her to be. I was stunned to see how different she seemed in her father's presence, as if a veil had fallen over her face.

Her father was catching the red-eye back to the East Coast, so we drove him straight from the restaurant to the airport. As we headed back home, my friend still seemed tense and withdrawn. Then suddenly she burst out, "I'll never match up to my father! He doesn't see me at all, and I don't think he ever will."

I found that to be an extraordinary statement. She wasn't a neuroscientist, she was an artist. Why on earth would she be trying to match up to her father? I bluntly asked her why she thought she had to compete with him at all. She said, "You don't know what it is like to be raised with such a powerful father who gets so much attention. Wherever you go, you are this man's daughter, not yourself. It makes you question your own abilities. It makes you doubt who you really are."

I asked her if her father ever acknowledged her for the wonderful art that she did. "Barely," she said. "He'd much rather see me happily married with a few kids." She said it matter-of-factly, but it was clear that the incident had touched a very painful place in my friend's heart.

I didn't want to drop her off at her house yet, so we went back to my house and sat on the couch. And there, now that this painful place had opened up, she cried her eyes out. I didn't try to make her feel better, because I realized that what she really needed was a safe place to let her pain out. Instead, I lit a fire and poured us each a little glass of cognac to relax with by the fireplace. I shared with her the work I had done to disentangle my own identity from my father's and how long it took me to understand that I was not his caretaker. And then I listened, because this was clearly an issue that she had to work through in her own way: to acknowledge her uniqueness and talent, and at the same time accept her father for himself. Maybe her father was never going to give her the kind of recognition she wanted, and maybe he would never really see her for who she was. That might not be what she wanted, but it wouldn't stop her from expressing her gift.

Finally, I asked my friend why she had never told me any of this before. She said, "It was too painful, and I was too ashamed. I couldn't admit it even to myself."

Ultimately, the deepest pain in our hearts comes from the things we hold against ourselves, when our hearts ache from the judgments we make. It's not just that we have disappointments and hurts; it's that we judge and reproach ourselves for them. It's not that we carry excess weight; it's that we make ourselves feel so wrong for carrying the weight. It's not that we're in a relationship we have outgrown; it's that we hold the change against ourselves. The critical voice in our heads tells us that there's something wrong with us. My friend thought there was something wrong with her because her father didn't value her accomplishments. For years, my mother held herself at fault because she had picked a man who was unfaithful to her, a man who wasn't the responsible, caring husband she would have wanted. She told herself that she should have known better, that she had made a huge mistake marrying this man she really loved. She blamed herself. As painful as the failed relationship was, that was her greatest heartache—the judgment on herself and him.

It can be very subtle how it works on us, this against-ness of self. We may not realize how we're binding our hearts when we judge ourselves for the way we feel or the way we are. But it's like wearing an undergarment covered in mud: anything we put on over it is going to feel sticky and dirty. We owe it to ourselves to invoke compassion and free ourselves from those judgments. And to do that, we need to feel our pain, cry our tears, and forgive our faults. This is a sure way to get through the painful places within us and come out safely on the other side—to come back to ourselves released and renewed.

CHAPTER 23

1-800-GO-INSIDE

Not long ago, a friend of mine was telling me how hard she found it to be with her mother. "Why?" I asked.

"My mother has no inner life," she replied, "and having a conversation with her is exhausting."

I was brought up by a mother who was basically one big inner life, so this was really foreign to me. "Tell me more," I encouraged my friend.

She began to describe a woman so outwardly focused that her "conversation" consisted of a constant commentary on the things and people around her. She wouldn't inquire into what anyone else was thinking or feeling, or discuss ideas or world events, and when people did share something about themselves—their feelings or their thoughts—rather than listening she'd be focusing on why their jackets were unbuttoned. She'd say things like "Your dress is too short" or "The people next door bought new garden furniture" or "Did you hear what happened to Anne's car?" She'd even ask what you were going to have for dinner while you were still having lunch. She was always picking apart the outward experiences of the world, instead of having her own ex- perience *in* the world. I could imagine how that would be utterly exhausting—for her and for my friend.

When I asked my friend why she thought her mother was so preoccupied with externals, she said that her mother was probably in so much pain that looking within was just too hard. I believe this is a common situ- ation, and the reason why many of us go around looking for the external fix, avoiding the real experience of our hearts.

How, then, do we go inside ourselves, when it's dark in there and the voices are too chaotic and grim? Don't you wish we could just pick up the phone and dial 1-800-GO-INSIDE? And then the recording would say, "For unresolved anger, resentment, or betrayal, press one. For not-good-enough or low self-esteem, press two. For loneliness, isolation, or shut-down emotions, press three. For stuck and not knowing where to begin, please stay on the line."

Such a service might not exist—but in fact, the line to our heart is always open. We just have to call. Explor- ing painful memories and false perceptions that block us from loving ourselves is a good start. Going inside is an ever-evolving process that requires a tremendous capac- ity for compassion.

My father, who had survived the wartime concen- tration camps, had a very mercurial personality and an erratic temper with unpredictable flares. He turned to all his senses to find fulfillment: an active extramarital sex life, business deals that came and went, a love affair with gambling, and a night life with lots of drinking. But he also had a brilliant intellect and the soul of a poet.

Toward the end of his life, when he got sick with diabetes, this led to macular degeneration, causing his eyesight to deteriorate so that he couldn't read or write. Those had been two of his great passions. He would often say to me that he was looking forward to having time to read and write—all the time he wanted—in his later years. Now the thing that kept him going had been taken away, and he was devastated. Desperate to find some help, he struggled with all sorts of optical devices, but though he could see light, he could not distinguish forms. Because he could no longer see out, he was *forced* to go inside—and inside him was a neglected garden that had not been watered or weeded for a long, long time. My father was often affectionate and tender, but the gate to his heart was closed. If we could read the sign on the gate, it would probably say: *No Entry—Explosive Materials Inside.*

It's not hard to see how my father lost access to his heart. The hurt and rage he took with him from the camps, along with the guilt of surviving when so many of his friends died, put the gate across his path. Different gates have different signs: judgments, blame, unmet expectations, crushed dreams, doubt as to whether there's anything in there worth loving at all. Feeling unworthy is one of the most common human conditions. It keeps us from knowing our true self, the one that lives in our inner world behind that forbidding gate.

We all struggle to let the gate open. We are all holding on to something that separates us from our heart.

But if we can go inside and find that something—and it takes courage to reveal it to ourselves, recognize it, and heal it—we may discover that our hearts are always accessible. It takes a shift in awareness and a willingness to let go. If we can let go of whatever holds us back from loving ourselves just the way we are—all of our faults, all those thoughts that undermine us, all those feelings of not being good enough—the gate will open all by itself.

I always saw my father as a mighty king trying to find his kingdom—a king with a poet's soul. There were brief moments when he would let his guard down, let his gate open a little. Then the richness of who he was would shine through, and his majestic presence would illuminate us—which made it all the more difficult to see the gate close again. And I can only imagine how difficult it must have been for him. I wish that once he had gotten inside the garden, he could have propped the gate so that it would stay open forever.

When we love someone, we so want to be there holding that gate open—but each of us has to lift the latch for ourselves.

CHAPTER 24

YOU'RE JUST PRETTY, YOU'RE NOT BEAUTIFUL

My mother had a habit of calling things the way she saw them. She didn't give much attention to what people thought of her, and her way of telling the truth was very . . . well, uncensored. And sometimes when she did this in my presence, I fervently wished that I were not there.

A dear friend of mine in L.A., an entrepreneur who was always chasing the next deal, had met and started to date a French woman who was rather wealthy and very glamorous, the daughter of a well-known Hollywood producer. She was considered very beautiful, and she obviously knew it. She walked around with an aura of superiority, hardly acknowledging anybody else's existence or extending an ounce of herself to anyone. She was, in a word, a snob.

One evening a group of us were going to dinner, and my friend brought this woman along. We started out with drinks at my house, and when they walked in, in walked her pretentious air right along with them. It was as if they'd brought a third person along—one who took up a lot of space and was not good company at all!

As we sat and talked, my mother came in with a tray of spanakopita, her traditional appetizer of spinach in phyllo dough. She went around the room, offering the hors d'oeuvres and exchanging a few warm words with everyone. Most of them knew her, and those who didn't were delighted to make her acquaintance.

Then she got to the French mademoiselle. She, of course, refused the spanakopita. My mother extended her hand and said, "Hello, I am Elli, Agapi's mother," at which the other woman nodded and made a sort of glottal sound.

My mother held on to the woman's hand and looked at her with a piercing gaze, as if she were at that very moment unmasking her. "Yes, you are very pretty," she said to her, right in front of everybody, then paused, still holding her hand. "But not beautiful. I will not give you beautiful. Beautiful is a whole other quality that you don't possess."

That was one of those moments where I might have liked the earth to swallow me up. I felt a chill down my spine and a knot in my stomach, but at the same time a wave of happiness that someone had found the courage to puncture this woman's facade. Somebody had to tell her, but since it wasn't going to be me, I'm glad my mother did. She had that kind of caring, that she would risk disapproval to reveal a moment of truth.

What I've discovered is that attitudes like our mademoiselle's often mask deep insecurities and tightly bound hearts. And underneath that, there is simply fear. What my mother had done was to see through the veil of aloofness that this woman had drawn around herself to cover whatever she was afraid to let the world see.

This is the danger of glamour: it makes us disguise what we are behind a mask of what we think we should be. It leads us to compare ourselves with others in a competition we can never win: there is always going to be someone more beautiful, more talented, more famous, richer, thinner, smarter, younger—and there is only one of you. So who is doing the measuring? If this is how you determine your value, eventually you will lose.

In the 21st century, we have turned beauty and fashion into gods in and of themselves—and we've done the same with money, art, politics, and even religion and spirituality. Instead of these things serving us, enhancing our lives as they were first intended to do, we are now bound to serving *them* as they dictate to us how we should live and how we should be. Movies, magazines, and advertisements hold up an artificial ideal that we can't possibly match. We judge ourselves against this ideal, which is really just an illusion; we give that illusion such power over us that we cannot accept ourselves as we are. Instead, we create conditions: *I need to have the perfect hips. I need to have the perfect lips. I should be a dress size smaller and a bra size bigger. I should look like* she *does*—whoever we've put on the pedestal for the moment. We're not at peace with those parts of our-selves just the way they are. I once heard a woman priest give a wonderful sermon called "Make Peace with Your Thighs" in which she talked about the importance of loving all parts of your body just as they are. I could have signed right up!

At the heart of our obsession with glamour lies the need to feel important. But important to whom? How important are we to ourselves? When the lights go out and the music stops and the glitter fades, it's us alone with ourselves, just our own light and our own shadow. How do we feel then about the beauty that's in us?

Beauty should enrich us, not enslave us. If we feel unattractive, imperfect, or simply insecure, then beau-tifying ourselves is an act of masking and covering up. But when we know the beauty of our real self and choose to reflect it in the way we wear makeup or jewelry or clothes, then it's an act of creativity and self-expression to amplify an inner radiance—not disguising what we are, but adorning it for all to see. The archetype of Aph-rodite, the goddess of glamour if ever there was one, ex-udes a quintessential beauty that's not bound by size, age, or fashion, and you always know this beauty when you see it. I don't know if you've ever seen ancient stat-ues of Aphrodite, but they don't fit our 21st-century ideal! She had a rounded belly and voluptuous hips; she was real.

I was leading a workshop once on the archetypes, and one of the participants was a nun in her 70s— a nun who was not cloistered and not wearing the habit. She arrived in shorts and a sleeveless shirt, carrying herself lightly and comfortably. In the same group there was also a former *Playboy* model. The model came in loaded down with issues about beauty, sexuality, and self-image; we all sensed how burdened she was. The nun, however, exuded joy and freedom. The beauty of her spirit was coming through in her body, and it shed light on everyone around her.

CHAPTER 25

TAKE CARE OF
YOUR CAPITAL

When we lived in Athens, we had a dear family friend who had known me and my sister since we were little girls. He lived in Thessaloniki, the cosmopolitan capital of northern Greece, where my mother was from. He was a classically warm, exuberant, generous Greek man, the kind we wish we could import more of into the U.S.! Whenever he came to Athens, he would visit us, and we all looked forward to his visits, which usually included bringing our favorite Greek sweets—baklava, melomakarona cookies, and tsoureki, the traditional sweet braided bread. This man was a very successful contractor, married to a very difficult, demanding woman who always seemed to be complaining about something.

One time he came to visit us after we hadn't seen him in some time. When he arrived at our apartment, he seemed out of breath after climbing the stairs to our door. It was clear that he was stressed and overworked; he looked run down, and he had put on weight. But when we sat down to dinner, he told us how well things were going in his life. He was thrilled about a new contract he had just won, to build a new museum in Thessaloniki. My mother listened for a little while without comment. Then she said to him, "I don't care how well your business is doing—you're not taking care of *you*. You're smoking, you're eating fatty foods, you're staying up late and getting up early—you're going to end up with a heart attack!" She went on: "Your business might have a great bottom line, but *you* are your own most important capital. Banking involves both withdrawing and depositing. There are only so many withdrawals you can make from your bank account, and you just keep on withdrawing. You could go bankrupt if you don't make some deposits soon."

She was really shaking the poor man up. He had expected a nice dinner with friends, good food and pleasant conversation, lots of laughs, not lectures or warnings of impending doom! But my mother was just warming up to her topic. She asked him when he had last had a checkup, and he admitted it had been a while. Then she told him he should go and be checked by a cardiologist. "I'm fine, Elli," he said, laughing. "I've just been under a lot of pressure."

But to my mother this was no laughing matter, and she got right up from the table and made a call to her own doctor. Doctors in Greece become part of your family (especially when your family includes my mother!). They come to your house for dinner, you go to theirs, and it's perfectly acceptable to call them at home outside office hours. So my mother made an appointment for our friend to see her cardiologist the following day, right there in Athens. To his surprise, though not to hers, they found that he had blocked arteries and needed to be admitted to the hospital right away for an angioplasty. My mother had more than likely saved his life.

A few years later, when the museum was finished, my mother got a package in the mail. It was the catalog of the museum's first exhibition, inscribed: *To Elli, who helped me remember what my real capital is.*

"Take care of your capital": that's what my mother would say anytime she saw us being pulled in too many directions, depleted by inner and outer demands. It was her favorite phrase when she needed to remind us to take care of ourselves; she meant that the smartest investment you could make was investing in your self. That profound metaphor still echoes in me now. How we conserve, spend, or invest our energy on a daily and even a moment-to-moment basis defines our lives. We have a responsibility to be good custodians of our gifts.

It's not always as obvious as it was with our family friend, who was letting his capital dwindle so dangerously. In my case, I had to learn to "take care of my capital" by finding out how I was affected by energy that wasn't mine. I'm a natural caretaker, and fulfilling others' needs is a very easy way for me to expend energy. As I realized how being a caretaker was depleting me, I had to become extremely conscious, disciplined, and vigilant.

I had to learn where I ended and where others began. At first I didn't know why I would walk into a room feeling fantastic and within 10 or 15 minutes find myself feeling completely deflated. I didn't know how I could be having a perfectly ordinary conversation with some-one and suddenly feel as if the wind had been taken out of my sails. I had to discern the boundaries between me and other people and understand that others' emotions, difficulties, processes, experiences—whatever they were going through—belonged to them, not to me. The more I "took care of my capital," the better an asset I became to those I cared for and to the world around me.

What does it really mean to take care of ourselves? How do we find where our energy is leaking? Where do we start? Sleep! My mother was very big on sleep. Sleep was sacred to her. If somebody was sleeping, there was nothing in the world that would make her interrupt that sleep. To her, it was a big investment in capital. You would reap the profits when you were awake. Whenever one of us came to her with a problem that needed solv-ing, small or big, she wouldn't feel pressure to come up with an instant answer; she would simply say, "Let it marinate overnight." She regarded sleep as a way that our consciousness worked out stress and found solutions to problems in our waking life.

Food! Food was another important investment in my mother's portfolio. When we were young girls in Ath-ens, there were long, delicious meals after school when we sat at the kitchen table and talked over the day. It was a time for us to unwind and reconnect over stuffed cabbage leaves, feta cheese, and tsoureki. My mother abhorred the whole notion of fast food so prevalent in America; to her, there should be nothing fast about food. When she saw people gobbling their food or eating on the run, she would say, "You're eating mechanically." She always reminded us that eating is meant to be a rit-ual, a way of communing with others and nurturing the body and soul. If she were alive today, she would regard as sacrilege the practice of keeping a BlackBerry on the table and checking e-mails or texting throughout a meal.

And then there was time out for your body and soul: my mother brought yoga and meditation into our lives from the time we were teenagers to help us learn to breathe, relax, and understand the value of centering ourselves. Of course, when you are 13, the thought of cultivating stillness is not exactly your idea of a good time, but my agile body took very easily to doing headstands.

Friendships: my mother knew that they can pay dividends or they can put you in the red. She knew how to distinguish between the givers and the takers and those who were impoverished at heart. She taught us how true friendships recharge us and renew us. She knew that energy follows thoughts—some thoughts bring us down, others lift us up. Good friends know us well enough to catch us when our thoughts are spiraling downward, and they help us reflect our better nature. It's so easy to close ourselves off in the world in order to protect ourselves. My friendships are a big part of keeping my heart open, giving me a safe place where I can be vulnerable. There, at our own little kitchen table, as we listened to each other's stories of the day, I learned the sacredness of a safe place. For years, my mother and my sister and I were like riverbanks for each other, providing a protected channel to flow into the world.

Sometimes it's easier to be generous with others than with ourselves—but being kind and compassionate with ourselves always gives a great return on our investment. Life can be so much more purposeful when we make ourselves a priority. This is not to be confused with self-indulgence; so many of our difficulties arise because we don't think enough of ourselves to take care of ourselves first. There's a wonderful quote that I love—"Treat yourself as if you were someone inexpressibly dear to you." Why would we expect others to treat us better than we treat ourselves?

A dear friend of mine was hugely overweight. We took a trip to Greece together with a group, and on the trip her knees gave out. She couldn't walk around with the rest of us; she couldn't climb the steps to the Acropolis or go any of the other places the group went, the places she had come to Greece to see. It was very painful for her, and for the rest of us who loved her, it was painful to witness. But the choice to take care of herself was up to her. She realized that she could either say, *This is the way I'm going to live*—or she could *live!*

This beautiful woman was in a marriage that no longer sustained her, with grown children who were off living lives of their own. Where was she to turn? She had to make the decision all on her own to treat herself with kindness and to take her life back into her hands—a decision that, after so many years of self-neglect, took tremendous courage to make.

It took my friend a year to lose 200 pounds, leave her marriage, start living on her own, and there, with no distractions, build the strength to care for herself. With help from a good doctor and good friends, she started a serious medical program that helped her drop the weight. Now, at the age of 60, she has built a rich, wonderful life, and it shows everyone around her that everything is possible once you decide that you are worth your own attention, loving, and care.

The beauty of this decision is that it frees you to take care of others as well. It lets you operate from a heartfelt, centered place, where you allow other people the freedom to be exactly who they are, just as you allow yourself. Your caring then can flow out to others from abundance, not from having to tip the cup over to get the last drop. And when you are taking care of your capital in this way, you can walk into a room full of chaos and keep your balance, knowing that you can give of yourself without giving yourself away.

CHAPTER 26

THERE IS NOTHING TO FIX

Some time ago I was on a plane on my way to one of my favorite cities, New York. Next to me, my beloved niece was immersed in her book. I was partly reading *Women Food and God*, while *fully* enjoying my chocolate ice cream and partly watching *Mary Poppins* on my iPod. That movie always evokes a magical sense of breaking the rules imposed on us, and the sight of a few good men dancing on the rooftops just delights me.

I love flying. I can be so free and so focused on a plane—I can read voraciously, write freely, organize anything, meditate for hours—or just sit and be. I love that feeling of being so far above the earth, no gravity weighing me down. I am not in control, and I can do no wrong; someone else is responsible for getting us there.

There is nothing I have to do but relax and enjoy the ride. If only I could capture that feeling on earth!

Ever since I was a little girl, I used to play a game with myself when I flew. Whenever the plane hit turbulence and the ride got bumpy, I would say, *If we don't crash, then when we land I will . . .* and then I would fill in the blank. At first, it was *I'll do better in math.* Later, *I'll be more organized, I'll clean my desk, I'll be kinder to myself, I'll take up singing again,* and so on. Then, of course, we would land safely, and I'd go on exactly as before. I very rarely implemented any changes I'd promised myself up in the air where everything seemed possible. Gravity always got the better of me.

For years, I looked at myself through the prism of trying to "fix" myself. It was subtle, out of sight, like a current underneath the smooth surface of a river, but it was altering the flow of my life—and of my loving. I tried to fix the people around me and to fix their behavior so that they'd fit into my idea of perfection. Once, I was in a relationship with someone who, it seemed, could do no right. And because he loved me so much, I thought it gave me carte blanche to make my adjustments on him. It happened so often that it became a joke. Whenever he did something I didn't like, I would say, "Darling, bear with me—I'm about to fix you." Of course, it was much more trying for me than it was for him, because trying to fix someone is exhausting! I was able to make a joke of it in that case, but in other situations, sometimes I wasn't even aware I was doing it. I was just going along with my underlying sense that things and people in their present state were somehow wrong and I needed to make them right—including myself.

From my earliest school days, one of my greatest challenges was fitting into the rigid structures that the world imposed. From the rigorous logic of equations in math class to the coursework in my master's program, where assignments had to follow prescribed templates that I found severely limiting, the need to conform was ever-present and often excruciating. My creative nature felt stifled. And I judged myself when I did not conform, even when I was doing something I was very good at. For example, if I made baklava and someone asked me for the recipe, I'd say, "You eyeball it," but they'd want to hear *six tablespoons of butter, half a cup of chopped nuts* . . . "Agapi," they'd say, "how can you not know how much butter to use?"

For a long time I felt that I did not fit within the structured, linear world, and this caused me tremendous distress. But while linear ways of doing things sometimes eluded me, creative expression was second nature: dance, drama, anything that took me to another magical plane. Daydreaming came very easily to me, and eventually I realized that daydreaming was actually calling me toward a different way of being, one that wasn't necessarily the world's way, but uniquely my own. When I started to find my own way, other things fell into place too, and I discovered that the structure I'd struggled with could actually be an ally, supporting my creativity and my life. The day that I accepted my true nature was a happy day.

The fact is, none of us really fits in. Nine out of ten people probably feel they don't fit in, and the tenth person just hasn't noticed yet! And we expend great amounts of energy trying to fix the parts of ourselves that don't conform so that we *will* fit in. But when you give up fixing yourself, first you start to fit comfortably in your own space, and then you discover that there's a whole world out there ready to receive you.

In different phases of our lives, this pattern shows up over and over again, as our ideas of what we should be and what our world should be differ from our changing reality. We women face this in a very primal way in our own bodies as they change with menopause. I thought it would never happen to me, the change of life, as they call it: the hot flashes, the fatigue, the shifts in body shape and weight and mood. But it started to hit me earlier in my life than I expected. I remember having a vivid dream one night that I was driving my car and it was out of control. That's really what it felt like. I didn't know what was happening to me at any level—emotional, mental, or physical—and it shook me to my core.

As my body changed, I started to feel that there was something wrong with me, and so I sought out doctors who I thought could fix me. One of the remedies I tried was a hormone-replacement therapy that backfired badly: the doctor gave me too much estrogen, and my breasts went up two cup sizes and my whole body started to bloat. Not exactly the result I was hoping for! Because your metabolism changes as well in menopause, I had more cravings than ever, and of course I turned to food for comfort—carbs and wine, which are the last things you need if you want to keep your energy up and your body functioning well. Perhaps the hardest part was seeing myself go from a size 8 to a size 12, thinking that there was something terribly wrong with being a size 12. The problem wasn't the size, it was my judgment about the size. One day I was putting on a pair of Spanx—those body-squeezing undergarments that smooth out your curves under your clothes—struggling with the tight stretch fabric and feeling frustrated and furious that I could not get my body back, when suddenly it dawned on me what I was doing. I said to myself, *It's one thing to put Spanx on your tummy, but you're putting Spanx around your heart!*

From then on, I surrendered. I accepted that this was a natural progression, one that required a lot of loving and a lot of kindness. And once I admitted that I couldn't "fix" me, help started to come to me from all directions. Friends who had experienced the change shared solutions that worked for them. New doctors helped me get the balance of hormones right to keep my body comfortable as it changed. Alternative practitioners helped me find the right kind of exercise and food and natural remedies, not to fix anything, but to help my body find its new balance. Most important, the changes in my body helped to dislodge the conviction that I had to look a certain way and be a certain way in order to feel good about myself. I had wanted *me* back, the way I was, but it turned out that the only way to get myself back was to move myself forward into the new phase, with all its gifts and challenges and new awareness.

I look at my life differently now, thinking in terms of what needs to be *healed* rather than *fixed*. I know that our attempts at fixing are bound to fail, because they are based on judgment—the judgment that something is wrong with the way things are, the way we are. We can course-correct, we can grow and learn, experience and explore, discover and discern what's right for us and what is not. But there is nothing to fix. Like the world around us, we are perfectly imperfect just the way we are.

CHAPTER 27

TAKING OFF
THE BAND-AID

A few years ago, a dear friend of mine was going through a complicated divorce. Since I was very close to her, I became completely immersed in her emotional situation even though I was working hard on deadline for my second book. When friends asked me how I was doing, I almost wanted to say, "I am going through a divorce." Then I remembered I wasn't even married!

This tendency to identify with other people's feelings is cultural. We Greeks are tribal; we empathize with each other, we become each other's therapists, and we are there for each other, mind, body, and soul. When my mother was going through her angst about my father's affairs, one of her dear friends would stay up night after night listening to the stories. I could hear her say, "Elli, you've told me this story a hundred times." But my mother needed to tell it a hundred more to get past the pain. Later in her life, she would know what to say to someone who was stuck in that way: "Darling, change the channel." But I see now that her wisdom and freedom were the result of all she went through on her own journey.

It's a wonderful gift to have caring family and friends to listen to you. When life gets turbulent, they can be a safe haven where you feel protected and embraced. However, when we internalize other people's problems and take on their pain as our own, then no one is being helped. I cared a great deal about my friend and was concerned about the outcome of her situation. I felt unhappy to see her suffer. But I was having a hard time finding the balance between being there for her and being there for my book. I had taken my cultural tradition to the extreme, and it wasn't working.

As you may know by now, taking on someone else's emotions was second nature to me. I didn't really know how it was possible to love and care for someone without identifying in that way. Recognizing this familiar pattern, I decided to investigate the situation. I asked myself, like a good reporter, "When did that pattern begin?"

It's interesting how, when we take the time to dialogue with ourselves, the answers start to be revealed. A particular incident surfaced from my memory: I was seven years old and a friend of the same age came over to my house to play. She fell and scraped her knee, and my mother placed a Band-Aid over the wound. The girl began crying, saying, "I don't want that Band-Aid!" My mother turned to me and said, "Why don't you put on a Band-Aid as well? That will make her feel better." Which of course I did. I liked my friend and I wanted her to feel better so she could play with me. When you are seven, you think, *Wow, if that's all it takes, if my putting on a Band-Aid can make my friend feel better, I'll do it!* Little did I know that the Band-Aid was going to leave a big imprint on me.

When I remembered this, I saw how, over the years, instead of letting my joy and well-being infuse other people, I had gone in the opposite direction and allowed other people's emotional states to become mine. I immersed myself in their feelings, making myself responsible for their happiness or lack of it. But as I reflected on it, I realized that I wasn't serving anybody by putting a Band-Aid on myself so that their wounds would hurt less. That was an irrational belief that I had to dismantle and a bad emotional habit that I had to break. I had to reclaim my right to be happy even when people around me whom I cared about were not. It was time to take off the Band-Aid.

So I had this resolution to take off the Band-Aid—I just had to figure out how. The habit of being too empathetic was so deeply ingrained that I needed to work at finding another way. One day I was driving my car after visiting my friend, feeling sad about this situation of hers that seemed so awful and all-consuming, and the thought came to me, *In a year or so it won't be as painful as it is now.* Then I realized that in five or ten years it probably wouldn't matter much at all. And in the year 3005, it *really* wouldn't matter, because none of us would be around! I was gaining a higher perspective—and it occurred to me that the best thing I could do for my friend would be to share that perspective with her.

The thing was, I had it backward. I thought that getting attached to people's problems was the way to love them, and that if I placed distance between myself and their problems, I wasn't acting like a caring human being. But the highest form of caring is really to step back and give others space to go through what they have to go through. It's presumptuous to think that other people can't handle what they're given. We all have a lot more resources than we know.

This has been one of the most challenging patterns for me to break. If over-empathizing with other people truly helped them, it might not be such a bad trait, but in my experience, it doesn't fix a thing. They're still going through it, and now you are, too. It's very liberating to find out that just loving people is enough.

When I talk to people about my Band-Aid metaphor, it's a great comfort to me to realize that a lot of them can relate! I think it is a very deep female trait. We see other people's unhappiness, and we ask ourselves, *What right do I have to be happy when my friend isn't?* For me, learning to claim that right is a lifelong process. When I find myself in situations of tension, conflict, or angst, I have to remind myself that I do not have to put on a Band-Aid to make the person who's hurting feel better. We all go through different cycles in our lives. But we have a choice: we can be compassionate and empathetic while still honoring the emotional state we ourselves inhabit. We all have the inner grace to help ourselves in what we're going through. The day I realized that, I felt a huge burden lift from me.

I had a heart-to-heart talk with my friend about her situation and mine, and we made a pact: whenever we got together, we would do things that were uplifting. I went with her to the gym, I took her to my favorite Greek restaurant, we volunteered together at her children's school. When she needed to express sadness or anger about the things that were going on, I listened, but I didn't collapse into sadness with her. I made sure we found things to laugh about and ways to let the feelings go. And when I had to immerse myself in my book and go for days without seeing her or talking to her, I didn't feel that I was letting her down.

Today, my friend is flourishing. She's done with the divorce, she has a new relationship in her life, and she has found a whole new strength to re-create herself. It takes a higher perspective to be able to see that this kind of transformation can happen and that these experiences, which seem so defeating in the moment, are there to serve a higher purpose.

CHAPTER 28

MY CONVERSATION WITH SOCRATES

"Know thyself." This famous saying by one of my favorite Greek philosophers, Socrates, has echoed through the ages. It is simple yet profound. These two words have been engraved on the archways of universities and the hearts of countless seekers of knowledge, and it's a motto that most of the self-actualized world tries to live by.

Socrates left it up to us to identify who this "self" is. We have so many selves that call for our attention. Our physical self wants comfort, food, security, and a pleasant home; our emotional self wants to know it is loved, wants to be heard, to be touched, and to express its feelings. Our mental self wants stimulation, information, knowledge, and conversation, and our worldly self wants recognition, stability, and money in the bank.

Then there's our spiritual self, which wants to be free to create, give, and serve, and to let go of anything that separates us from one another or divides our own hearts. So, Mr. Socrates, what self are we to be true to, and at what time? And how do we find our truth in the midst of all the selves that are pulling us in so many directions?

The Socratic method was to ask questions that would guide students to answers. I had some questions of my own—and since I've always believed that all of us are connected, even across space and time, I realized I could just ask him directly!

I caught up with Socrates on a busy Athenian street to get his thoughts on this most pressing question: What self was it? As he strode along and I hurried to keep up, this is what he said:

"Know thy self, and I mean *all* of it. Your true self and your false self. Get to know it all—the doubt, the shame, the guilt, the lack and the self-pity, the lust and the jealousy, the greed and the pride. It's part of your human nature. And let the other parts of your self, the kindness, loving, compassion, clarity, and wisdom, come through. There is a fearlessness that lives in you. When fear takes over, ask yourself, 'Who is afraid in there?'" And he added, "I know about fearlessness, because I didn't give a damn what people thought of me, neither did I think of pleasing X, Y, or Z. At the very end, I didn't even fear death. They threatened me with death when they condemned me to drink the hemlock; I challenged them and asked them, 'How do you know that death is worse than what is here?' They didn't! Nobody does.

"To know thyself is also to meet yourself in the unknown, the invisible, the unspoken. Take time to let that speak to you. Leave spaces in your busyness for that silent, true self to be heard. And don't listen too closely to what your false self tries to whisper in your other ear. Your false self is the master of distortion. It throws out hooks and you bite, and then it reels you in and has its way with you. It pulls you down paths that are not your own, and you feel wobbly on them, as if you were walking in someone else's shoes.

"The real self patiently watches you until you step aside to let it lead. You may connect with it in a moment of silence or in a moment of listening to someone else. You may find it when you speak your truth against all odds, or when you're doing something ordinary, like cooking a meal or cleaning the floors or taking a walk. When you are there for someone who has less than you, when you hear more than what people are saying, when you take off the mask of your image—that is when the true self shows its face."

"Then, Socrates," I asked him, "how do you really know which is the real you and which are the parts you've adopted to survive?"

"You become like a detective," he replied. "You become an investigative reporter. When you feel separate or petty or abandoned or lacking in this or that, when you feel angry or empty, when you compare yourself to those you think are more fortunate, when you want to lash out at the world for all it's not bringing you—then ask yourself, like a good reporter: 'Who exactly is feeling that in there? And where did you come from? How long have you lived there? Who gave birth to you? Who are your friends?' In this way, find out all you can about those parts that are like little weeds that choke your heart and stop its joy. Be sure to listen to the answers, but be careful. If you judge, criticize, or make those parts wrong, you'll be trapped by them. Why don't you just let them speak and then show them the door?"

Socrates was on fire. Marching on toward the agora, he carried on: "When I said that the unexamined life is not worth living, that is what I meant: questioning why you are the way you are. You are the keeper of the keys to yourself. You have the power to choose to know yourself by observing from a higher altitude, seeing all the things in you and around you. As you ask questions like a good reporter, investigating the world you see, it will reveal more and more of the world you do not see, the invisible world.

"Be the eternal student. Know the things you know and admit the things you do not know. Don't take things for granted. Ask the questions. When you go to sleep, ask where you go and who keeps your heart beating and who brings you through the night. Keep a journal by your side in case you get an answer. When you wake up, ask, 'Who woke me up?'—other than your alarm clock.

"Be in awe that you walk on the earth that revolves around the sun, right under your feet, as you walk to work wondering how your stocks are doing. Some other force is moving that earth and that sun and those feet. And as you get in the elevator, worrying about how your day will be, about meeting your deadlines and confronting your colleagues and whether your spouse still loves you and how your kids will get through school, wonder also at how all those things are connected and how you are connected to the whole.

"You'll start to see that you have choices, and you'll start to exercise your choices and experience your freedom. And guess what? At some point, other people will feel that freedom in you and want to be around you, because everyone—*everyone*—wants to feel their freedom. That is a grand service to your fellow humans. When you take care of yourself that way and honor yourself, you don't assume you're a lesser person just because you have some insecurities."

I stared at him, taking to heart all I was hearing. And then Socrates turned to me with the mischievous look of a loving teacher who could see through many illusions. "You think you are your insecurities?" he laughed. "For the gods' sake, woman—you are the miracle of life itself!" And then he strode away into the agora, where, now that he had raised my consciousness, he could go shake up a few more minds and hearts.

CHAPTER 29

THE GIFT OF FORGIVENESS

Toward the end of his life, my father stayed with us in Los Angeles for a while. The day he was leaving for Greece, we all knew he would not return. His health was failing. His bags were packed and the car was in the driveway, waiting to take him to the airport to catch a night flight to Athens. He had hugged all of us and said his goodbyes.

My sister, my mother, and I walked him to the car. As he was about to get in the car, he suddenly turned and reached for my mother's hands. Looking at her for what he knew would be the last time, he began to weep. "Forgive me, my Elli," he said. "Forgive me, Elli *mou.*"

My sister and I stood on the front steps of the house, holding each other, witnessing this moment in which so much pain was being released. My mother held my father's hands for what felt like an eternity. The tenderness was so palpable that I felt the very stones of the house could melt. She simply allowed him the gift of asking for forgiveness, and her silence spoke volumes of her acceptance.

I stood there in awe of what I was witnessing: a man whose life was about to end, acknowledging the hurt he had caused, and, in an act of surrender, taking an action of tremendous courage. Here was someone so strong—someone who, like Odysseus, had withstood the trials of a turbulent journey in both his outer and his inner life—now letting all his heart's defenses fall away. I know it was cathartic for my mother, who had loved him for all those years; through his apology, she was in some sense vindicated. But for my father, I think that moment was the great gift of his life. In asking forgiveness of my mother, he was really asking it of himself—and in that very moment of asking, it was granted.

Then we kissed my father once again and watched him drive away—me, of course, promising to visit him soon in Greece. As we walked my mother back into the house, I looked at her; she seemed radiant and peaceful, as if the hand of love had touched her face. When love releases in our body like that, it's as if the cells wake up from a deep slumber, from a numbness. Love pours out from our soul, flowing into our very cells. As I walked back into the house, I trembled with aliveness.

That moment gave me a new awareness of the impact that forgiveness can have. I saw it for one of the greatest gifts we can give, simply because it releases withheld love—love we've been keeping from others and from ourselves. Ultimately, if we want to feel more love in our lives—and who doesn't?—forgiveness is the surest way.

Forgiveness doesn't only apply to the big things, the hurts and betrayals. The issue can be as simple as a parking ticket. We forget to feed the meter, we get a ticket, and we judge ourselves: how could we be so careless? Then we forgive ourselves and let it go.

Forgive yourself for what you did or didn't do, for things that happened and things that didn't happen. Forgive yourself for what you think is going to happen in the future. Forgive yourself all the judgments you make about others when they don't act the way you want them to act; forgive the judgments you've made on your own life. Do this over and over again, because a loving spirit needs constant attention. You can wake up one day feeling fantastic, then you have a confrontation with your boss—or get that parking ticket—and down shuts the heart. So forgiveness is not a one-shot deal, it's a daily practice.

I'd like to tell you another story, this one about a dear friend who was in great pain over divorcing her husband. She had devoted her life to helping him succeed and to raising their two children—until he left her for his young secretary. Their divorce dragged on for years, and throughout that time my friend was haunted with betrayal, resentment, and a determination to get back at him somehow. She was miserable.

One day I took her to walk the labyrinth at a spiritual center in Los Angeles. A labyrinth is similar to a maze, except a maze is designed to get you lost, whereas the intention of a labyrinth is to bring clarity as you weave your way to its center on a path where you can't go wrong. In the tradition of the labyrinth, as you walk it, you pose a question to which you want an answer— something you need to resolve inside you.

My friend stepped into the labyrinth asking the question that was devouring her: *How can I get rid of my obsession with my ex and his new lady?* What she really wanted was to put down the burden of hurt she'd been carrying for so long.

When she reached the center of the labyrinth, she told me later, she saw her husband's face—she remembered and reconnected with the love that she had first felt for him. She suddenly had a clear realization that whatever he was doing in his life, she didn't have to be bound by it anymore. In a moment of grace, she let go.

The next day, as it happened, she had a court date to finalize the divorce proceedings. She walked in, calm and confident, free from turmoil. Her husband's lawyer stated what they were offering her as a settlement. She turned to her own lawyer and said, "Accept it."

Her lawyer looked at her in amazement. "What happened to you?" he said. "You came into this wanting to fight for everything!"

She answered peacefully amid the thick tension in the wood-paneled room, "I don't want to spend my time and energy fighting. I have had enough."

When she shared the news with me, we cried together. I sensed the liberation that she had found in her heart, and I was so grateful that I had been a part of it. That night we went to a Greek restaurant and made a toast to her freedom from the past. In the years to come, if residual pain resurfaced, she'd focus on forgiving again; but for now, she had wiped the slate clean.

CHAPTER 30

IT IS
DONE

Ever since my mother and my father separated when I was 12, I had taken it upon myself to be his sole (or perhaps "soul") caretaker. His life had been a roller coaster of successes and failures, addictions and passions—the gamut of human experience and human emotions. As a child, I felt all of that and wanted to ease his suffering. Even as an adult, when we were thousands of miles apart—when he lived in Athens and I lived in the United States—I felt a tremendous sense of responsibility, even over-responsibility, for him. In the latter part of his life, he was surrounded by the love of my sister, Arianna, and me, his grandchildren, and Michael, my brother-in-law, with whom he had an extraordinarily close relationship. Ironically, Michael didn't speak Greek and my father didn't speak English, so I always ended up being the translator between them. I felt like I was the net in a table tennis love match. My father had visited and stayed with us for a while in the States, but then he returned to Greece to finish his book about the history of Greece into modern times, as well as, really, to finish the last chapter of his life. At that time, I was living in New York, and I stayed in close contact with him.

My father suffered from diabetes, which had already made him nearly blind and was now taking its toll on the rest of his body. In the last year of his life, he would often call me, telling me that he was feeling really sick and thought he was going to die. I would think nothing of getting on a plane and going to Athens to be with him. Once I was there, our love and caring for each other would cheer him up and revitalize him, and he would feel better.

Early in May of 2000, I got another one of those calls. With his indomitable sense of humor, my father said to me, "I'm going to die—and this time, it's for real!" Of course, I found myself on a plane again. When I got there, I had a feeling he was right. His kidneys were failing, and every day he deteriorated a little more. He could get out of bed only with help, and he slept a lot. His doctor visited him every day, in the Greek tradition, and kept telling me that things didn't look good. We had a caretaker with him around the clock. I sat by his bedside, caressing his hand, reading to him, comforting him.

One night he asked me, "When do you have to be back in New York?" I told him I had to be back by May 12 because I had a performance to do. "That's okay," he said in his dry, humorous way, "because I'll be dead by then." I couldn't figure out how he would actually die;

although weak in his body, he seemed so present, so alert and alive in his mind.

A few days later, I left him to go to a Greek Orthodox monastery outside the city, in Thebes, to meet with a priest whom my father dearly loved. I stayed there for two days, meditating and praying for my father. On the second day, I got a call from his doctor, who told me that his kidneys had failed and he had to be sedated. I rushed back to be by his side, and I called my mother and Arianna immediately. Arianna was traveling for work, but she dropped everything to get on the next flight so that she could see him before he died. I knew the end was near.

Even sedated, he was still alert and asked me when Arianna was coming. I told him her flight landed at 9:02 A.M. the next day. He said, "Make sure, when you pick her up, to bring her gardenias and lilies." Those were the flowers he had always brought us when he welcomed us at the airport—his gesture of love and honor for his daughters.

That night, I lay next to my father for several hours, caressing his forehead and praying, being fully present in the love we had for each other. He kept saying to me, "You are my comforter, you've always been my comforter in my life." His breathing became heavier and heavier. Then, suddenly, I felt a most soothing, loving presence touch my hand. I heard a voice inside gently say, "It is done." I had made a promise that I would be with my father until his last breath, but now I sensed that my work was complete. It was time for me to leave him to take the last step on his own.

Feeling as if I were suspended between two worlds, I got up from his bedside and went into his office, where he stored pictures, papers, and letters. Surprisingly, I was completely at peace, knowing that my father was being delivered into Spirit's care. There was nothing else for me to do but start to let go.

I gathered up the letters, photographs, and objects that I knew mattered most to him, and then a friend gave me a ride back to my hotel. On the way, we stopped by the florist's and I got exactly the flowers he wanted me to buy for Arianna—gardenias and white lilies. When I arrived at my hotel, I ran a bath. I remember falling asleep in the tub, and when I woke up, grateful I hadn't drowned, I had the feeling that I had been in some other place, communing with my father. I felt total love and acceptance, all at peace. I didn't have a distinct memory, but I had a certainty that I had been with him in that other place. I looked at myself in the mirror and I felt how small my body was next to the largeness of the awareness I'd just experienced.

I headed to bed after my bath and fell into a deep sleep, to be awakened by the friend who was taking me to the airport to meet Arianna. As we drove to my father's apartment, we called his caregiver, Vicki, to check on him. I asked her, "Vicki, how is Daddy?" In a quiet, tender tone, she said, "He just died." He had passed away at the exact moment that Arianna landed—9:02 A.M.—part of the mystical, perfect master plan.

When we walked into his apartment, the windows were open and a gentle breeze was blowing through. The people from the funeral home had already come and prepared his body and dressed him in his suit. He was lying on his bed with candles around him, and he looked absolutely beautiful. And his presence was electrifying. Crying, Arianna and I sat by his bed and told him how much we loved him. It was remarkable—he was gone from his body but so present with us in his soul. In the midst of the loss, I had a great sense of a burden being lifted. His work was done.

I couldn't possibly think about logistics—but Arianna, in her amazing way, started to make arrangements. She said to me, "We are burying him tonight at the monastery, and we are leaving tomorrow for New York so you can be back for your performance. We're leaving everything else up to Vicki and her family. Anything we want, they will send to us in the States." And that is just how it happened.

We buried him that night at the monastery in Thebes in a beautiful Orthodox ceremony. Then we got up at 4:00 A.M. the next morning and drove from Thebes back to the airport in Athens. I cried all the way across the Atlantic; I couldn't stop the river of tears rolling down my face. The loss was beginning to sink in—the void where his presence and his love and his need for me had been. I cried not only for my loss but for the suffering he had gone through that I could never really take away, and I prayed that he would now find the comfort he had never found on this earth.

I did make it to my performance—though God only knows who performed—and then I flew back to L.A. as fast as I could to be in my mother's arms, to be with my family, and to grieve the loss. It was beautiful to see how truly my mother loved my father. After all the hard times there had been, all the separations, anger, pain—everything they went through together—it was a gift to see how her heart was still bonded with his. She was grief-stricken, and I'm sure that's what caused her heart to give way just a few months later.

I've often reflected on the words I heard when my father's life was coming to an end—*It is done*—and on the power of that concept. Whether it be the end of a relationship, the end of a job, or the end of a certain phase in our lives—and of course the biggest of all phases is our time of passing—these transitions can bring a tremendous peace if we are willing to surrender.

CHAPTER 31

Don't Miss the Moment

My mother died on August 24, 2000, exactly three and a half months after my father's passing. Their bond was so tight that when my father died, she was bereft, a woman who had lost the man she had so loved even after all she had been through with him.

While he was still alive, her heart was already weakening. We didn't know how serious it was until one night, nine months before she died, when she was sitting in our kitchen and began having intense pains in her limbs. We were terribly worried, but she didn't want us to call a doctor. She just kept putting on homeopathic ointments and taking aspirin for the pain. I was getting ready to go out to do a performance at the Getty Center to promote my new book, and my mother had planned to come, but she couldn't—the pain was too strong.

Normally she wouldn't miss anything that her daughters were a part of, so I knew she must really be suffering. Still, she was refusing to see a doctor; she wouldn't admit there was something serious going on.

A few days later, my book tour took me to Washington, where I performed at the National Museum of Women in the Arts. That night, at 4 A.M., I got a call from my sister. "Mummy is in the hospital," she said. "She has a staph infection that's gone into her bloodstream. We don't know if she'll make it."

I was terrified. I remember thinking, *I can't imagine a world without my mother.* She had been such a big part of my life that a world without her loving, her nurturing, her eccentricity, her originality, seemed a world that would be bereft of joy.

I took the next flight back to L.A. When I arrived at the hospital, my mother was in surgery as they tried to treat the infection. Two weeks before, she had cut her elbow; it became infected, but she wouldn't go on antibiotics. She kept trying to heal it in her own way. Now the infection had gotten into the blood and it was threatening her life. She stayed in the hospital for four weeks on heavy doses of antibiotics and sedatives. I never prayed so hard in my life. All our friends, all the people who loved her, were praying ceaselessly, too. It was so painful to watch her suffer, and I felt helpless to do anything about it.

During her stay in the hospital, while my father was still alive in Greece, he called her on the phone. They talked for an hour and a half. As she described it later, my father stepped in with his deep love for her and infused her with a sense of her own strength, conveying to her how she could overcome this, as she had so many other things in her life. That was a very significant call for her to receive, and it helped her get well enough to leave the hospital.

She came home, but she wasn't the same. She was fighting depression, sleeping a lot, and waking up without her bearings. In the hospital she had been diagnosed with congestive heart failure. It's so hard for the soul to reside in a body that is fighting a disease; it requires a tremendous amount of loving and care. We were fortunate and could have nurses for my mother around the clock so that she would take her medicines, eat her special foods, and be looked after with great care. But she didn't like being dependent on anyone for anything, even while her body was trying to heal. She still wanted to do things her way.

Over the spring and summer, she did regain some of her old energy. We were able to do things she loved, like walking on the beach. But I had the sense that she was wrapping up her time here on earth. In August she began to weaken, and we begged her to see her doctor, but she wouldn't go; she wanted *him* to come see *her*. "Come on your day off," she told him. "I'll cook for you." But this was not Greece, where doctors made house calls and visited their patients for dinner!

Finally we got her to the doctor, and she was quickly admitted to the UCLA hospital. Early the next morning, she suffered a minor stroke and they put her in the ICU. When we saw her, she looked like she was in a coma. The specialists told us that her brain had been damaged and she might not wake up.

We spent hours at her bedside, trying to figure out if there was anything more we could do. Arianna would hold our mother's hand and tell her that she loved her.

My nieces' caretaker, Maricela, who had looked after the girls since they were born and had become part of our family, came and massaged her feet and hands. She put a lemon in her hand, because my mother always loved lemons; she would boil them to make the house smell fresh, and she put them in everything she cooked. Then Maricela bent down close to my mother and said, "Miss Elli, if you wake up, I will take you to Ross: Dress for Less." My mother loved to go to Ross, the discount store, and stock up on presents so she'd have something to give whenever the opportunity arose. It gave her tremendous happiness to give unexpected presents to people. Would you believe it, at that she cracked a tiny smile. To the relief of all of us around her, a little ray of hope came in.

What happened next was nothing short of a miracle. She woke up as Lazarus had done in the Bible, as if she were raised from the dead, bright and filled with light, and we took her home. The day she came home, she sat on the patio in her little hospital gown, eating blueberries and offering them to all the people who came to see her. We felt as if the heavens had given us the gift of our mother back. It was a gift that would last only one week.

When my mother finally walked into her bedroom that first day, she looked around and said, "This is so strange. Where am I?" She was between two worlds—the physical world that was fading and the spiritual world that was opening. She had already been in that world, it was obvious. Looking after her that last week felt sacred, because I knew she could go at any moment. I massaged her, I held her, but I didn't want to say goodbye. I think when we love someone so much, we don't ever want to say goodbye. We don't want to be the ones to initiate that ending, so we wait until life thrusts it upon us and says, "It is done."

One morning near the end of the week, my mother said to me, "I want to go to the international food market in Santa Monica." That was like Disneyland for her; she'd leave with baskets full of food, fruit, and goodies for everyone. So I took her there. My mother in her fragile little body, still filled with a zest for life, bought salamis and cheese, olives, halvah, Viennese chocolate and Greek chocolate, and nuts, and by the end, we had bags and bags of food to bring back home. It was surreal taking her out into the world; there she was, like an apparition, buying food, and there I was, trying to hold the two realities together. I wanted to say to the checkout clerk, "You don't seem to understand what is happening here. This is my mother! And she's going! Can you please take care of her? Can you please take care of me?" But instead, I kept pretending that it was just like any other day. Deep down, I knew that we were shopping for the last supper, but I was holding it together so I wouldn't fall apart.

We went home, and my mother spread out the most amazing lunch in the kitchen, saying to me and our housekeeper and Arianna's office staff and whoever was in the house, "Sit now and let us enjoy our food!" It was a feast. I couldn't help thinking, *Look at her appetite for food and love and sharing! This is not a woman who is going to die!*

Early that evening, I came into her room and found her sitting at a little table, shelling shrimp and eating them. "Sit and eat some shrimp!" she said to me. She had her hair in little pigtails and she was playing beautiful Greek music. She was like a happy child. Now I know why she was so happy—because her spirit was calling her back and she was ready. There was no struggle, there was no suffering, there was simply grace.

Later on, I went out for a while, and Arianna and the girls stayed with her. When I got home, Arianna met me at the door. She said to me, "Mummy has just fallen. She's in the bathroom. She doesn't want us to call the paramedics. Should we call them anyway?"

I ran into the bathroom—really a large dressing room between the bath and the bedroom—and saw my mother on the floor, putting lavender oil on her feet. She said in a strong voice, "Do *not* call the paramedics. I'm fine." I felt so torn. One voice said, *She doesn't want you to call them,* and the other said, *If you don't call them she will certainly die,* back and forth, back and forth, reaching for the phone with one hand and putting it down with the other. So, instead of the ambulance, I called my mother's nurse, and she came right away. We all sat in the dressing room with my mother, her young granddaughters riding their scooters up and down the hallway, making happy noises, unaware of what was happening, because my mother was trying to keep everything and everyone calm. The nurse kept taking her pulse, but her pulse was fine. And even though I kept urging her to get up, she wouldn't. Instead, she asked me to open a bottle of red wine and pour glasses for everyone.

We all sat there, chatting and telling stories, for an hour or more, waiting for her to get up. There she was on the floor with a beautiful turquoise sarong wrapped around her, making sure we were all having a good time. It sounds surreal now, and it was surreal even then. I had the sense that something larger was moving all of us, keeping us from taking any action, so that my mother would have the chance to pass the way she wanted to pass. When I look back, it's as if Spirit was saying, *Relax—there's nothing you need to do. We've got her now.* Then suddenly her head fell forward and she was gone.

Later, I found out my mother had confided to the housekeeper that she knew she had suffered a stroke and her time had come. She asked her not to tell us, and the housekeeper, who had known and loved my mother for years, understood why and honored her wishes. My mother knew that we would insist on getting her to the hospital, and she didn't want to die in the hospital. She wanted to be at home, with her daughters and her precious granddaughters around her, in the warmth of those she loved and who loved her. She didn't want to miss the moment.

We scattered my mother's ashes in the sea with rose petals, as she had asked. And we gave her the most beautiful memorial, with music, friends, poetry, gardenias, and lots of food: a memorial that truly honored her life and her spirit. Everyone felt her presence there, taking part, looking down on us and shining her light on us. In our garden, we planted a lemon tree in her honor that has been producing juicy lemons ever since. And we installed a bench engraved with one of her favorite sayings that embodied the philosophy of her life: *Don't Miss the Moment.*

CHAPTER 32

COMING HOME TO ITHAKA

We were about to land in Athens on Olympic Airways. As the Athenian cityscape became more visible from the blue sky, I could feel the memory of my city and all the familiar emotions that it evoked from my childhood start to surface as well. And I felt a pang in my heart. It was the first time since my father died that I was coming back. Ten years had gone by, and I was now returning to do a documentary for PBS on the Greek gods—*Quest for the Gods,* it was called.

I was nervous about how it would feel without my father there to greet me—without his love to welcome and surround me during my stay. He had been the reason I kept going back, and the joy he had in seeing me always made the trip meaningful. And then, just as I was about to cover up my feelings, so as not to experience the loss and the vulnerability, he showed up.

I heard his strong and sweet voice as he said to me in Greek, *"Kalo ilthes agapi mou na perasis orea ke na xekourastis."* Oh yes, it was my father's presence. "Welcome, my darling. Have a good time and make sure you rest." That was what he always used to say to me. As an act of love, my father showed up in spirit to welcome me, and then I knew I was going to be fine.

And I was. The trip went great, and all sorts of miracles kept happening. The permits to shoot at the ancient monuments came through in a day. The famous ancient theater in Athens allowed me to perform there and be filmed while the Greek Theatre Festival was going on, which is unheard of. The magic of little miracles manifesting was unmistakable, and I felt my father's presence, like a canopy of love and affection above me.

Our last stop was Ithaka, island of Odysseus, the hero of Homer's epic poem *The Odyssey.* In the myth, Odysseus leaves his island to fight the Trojan War and then tries to get back home. For 30 years, the sea and the winds thwart him and try to break him, but after all the adventures and the struggles and the loss of his companions, he returns home to Ithaka, to his beloved wife, Penelope.

Constantine Cavafy wrote the modern poem "Ithaka" (you can read it following this chapter), describing so beautifully the odyssey that all of us go on in our lives and the obstacles we have to overcome on the way to discovering our true selves. He encourages us to enjoy the journey, not to hurry it, but to take pleasure in all the new sights and knowledge and riches we find along the way. "Keep Ithaka always in your mind," he says. "Arriving there is what you're destined for." But when you do arrive, don't expect Ithaka to give you anything more: Ithaka gave you the beautiful journey itself. "Wise as you will have become, so full of experience, you'll have understood by then what these Ithakas mean."

I had never been to Ithaka. It takes about nine hours to get there from Athens, six hours by bus and three by boat. We stayed at a charming little hotel by the port. We were going to shoot some of the scenes about Demeter there—the goddess of fertility and nurturing, the mother goddess. We had a feast prepared by some of the local people, up on the terrace of a house overlooking the bay, which we all noticed had the shape of an open heart. We shot the sequence in which I talked about the love Demeter had for her daughter and about her passion for the earth and its people.

That evening, filled with warmth and the magic of the land, I went back to our hotel and lay in my bed with the white chiffon curtains around me. The windows were open so the moonlight was shining in and the soft breeze was breathing into the room. I could smell wild jasmine and hear waves crashing against the seawall, and all at once I was filled with a sense of home. I felt I had come home to myself.

I started to let in a tenderness and a love for myself, and my heart opened a little more with gratitude for my journey. I became aware that the underlying pull I had felt throughout my life was a call from myself, guiding me back on course lest I miss myself along the way. Now there was no pull anymore, only a deep sense of connection that left me with tears streaming down my face. My heart reached out—to the moon, to the Aegean, to the land that I was born in, my first home, which was now bringing me back to the home inside me: a place, quite simply, of love.

At that moment, I made a promise to tell my story, so that my story might help others to remember that our true home is inside ourselves and that it is worth everything we go through to return there. And even when we think we have lost the way and the port is nowhere in sight, the loving part in us is waiting, loyal, and patient like Penelope, for our return home. That part is the compass that never loses its way, even when we do.

Before the inexplicable mystery of the universe, we are all the village fools. But in our choice to reveal our hearts to ourselves and to each other, we can all be masters and healers. We can be each other's pathfinders, hold the ladder for each other to climb higher than we can alone, open doors that we cannot open on our own, be each other's lighthouses on our journey home, and realize that we are safe and never alone. And then our life on earth can be transformed.

ITHAKA

C. P. CAVAFY

As you set out for Ithaka
hope your road is a long one,
full of adventure, full of discovery.
Laistrygonians, Cyclops,
angry Poseidon—don't be afraid of them:
you'll never find things like that on your way
as long as you keep your thoughts raised high,
as long as a rare excitement
stirs your spirit and your body.
Laistrygonians, Cyclops,
wild Poseidon—you won't encounter them
unless you bring them along inside your soul,
unless your soul sets them up in front of you.

Hope your road is a long one.
At many a summer dawn to enter
May there be many summer mornings when,
with what pleasure, what joy,
you enter harbors you're seeing for the first time;
may you stop at Phoenician trading stations,
to buy fine things,
mother of pearl and coral,
amber and ebony,
and sensuous perfumes of every kind,
sensual perfume of every kind—

as many sensual perfumes as you can;
and may you visit many Egyptian cities,
to learn and go on learning from their scholars.

Keep Ithaka always in your mind.
Arriving there is what you're destined for.
But don't hurry the journey at all.
Better if it lasts for years,
So you're old by the time you reach the island,
wealthy with all you've gained on the way,
not expecting Ithaka to make you rich.

Ithaka gave you the marvelous journey.
Without her you wouldn't have set out.
She has nothing left to give you now.

And if you find her poor,
Ithaka won't have fooled you.
Wise as you will have become, so full of experience,
you'll have understood by then
what these Ithakas mean.

ACKNOWLEDGMENTS

I have discovered the joys of unbinding my heart, but my heart is bound full of gratitude to the people who helped make this book possible. Every single one of them contributed their threads of support, encouragement, inspiration, enthusiasm, and valuable comments to help make the tapestry complete.

John Roger, my wonderful teacher and friend, has been a guiding light in my life, always helping me find my way to my own truth. When I told him I wanted to write this book, he encouraged me by saying, "You must tell your story because you never know who might read it out there and unlock something in themselves." For his presence, love, and friendship, I am and always will be deeply grateful.

Before this book became the book you're holding now, it sat for a long time in a big plastic box with the label "Heart book material—my next book." Then Jan Shepherd stepped in. Jan has been a dear friend for many years; she knew my mother and always wanted me to tell my mother's stories. She encouraged me to take the proposal out of the box and send it to the man who would become my agent, Bill Gladstone. Jan was my Greek muse/Jewish mama throughout the process, from reading every draft of every chapter—being truthful, urging me to speak in my true voice—to phone calls that started not with "How are you?" but with "How is the writing?" She was there from the start to the finish line. She is my treasured friend, and I'm deeply thankful to her.

Bill Gladstone, my dynamic agent, knew exactly what to do with the material that came out of the box. He helped me shape the proposal and find the perfect home for it—with Hay House and my editor, Patty Gift.

When I first heard Patty's voice on the phone, it was love at first sound. Our connection was instant; I felt I had come home. Her giving of herself, her authenticity, her brilliance in seeing what the book should be, and her caring to make it as vibrant and connected as possible, make her exactly what her last name says: a true gift. I am grateful for all she did to bring the book to life, and for having her in my life as my true friend.

Patty introduced me to Anne Barthel to help structure and edit the book. My heart leaped the moment I met her. Anne sings in a choral group, and the same spirit that makes singers part of an ensemble—getting themselves out of the way to serve the music—is what she brought to the material, along with her passion for language and form. She helped me appreciate that less is more—a real task for a Greek! She became a safe haven where I could write what was in my heart, and she made the normally onerous experience of editing and rewriting a joy. My love and gratitude go to her.

To my friends who are part of the book's family, a big thank you:

To my beloved friend Joan Witkowski, who is a constant source of love in my life, and whose insightful comments made each chapter crisper.

To Mastin Kipp, who told me that Hay House was the right home for my book when the book was just an idea, and then brought me to the lovely Lizzie Vance. Lizzie was instrumental in the first phase of the book: when I started to tell my story, she listened and took endless notes and helped me build the book's foundation.

To Brian Sirgutz, who was with me through the process, wholeheartedly supporting me in sharing my story.

To Harvey Karp and Nina Montee, whose thoughtful suggestions and abundant enthusiasm for the subject warmed my heart.

To Michael Hayes, whose love and support lifted my spirit and constantly reminded me not to lose perspective.

To Alicia Hayes, whose joy and support were invaluable.

To Nicole Avant, who encouraged me from the first glimpse of the idea with an unequivocal "Absolutely go for it!"

To Heide Banks, for her insightful comments and her ability to keep it fun throughout the process.

To Paula Reiser, for her thoughtful edits in the early stages.

To John Morton and Leigh Taylor Young, who were there from the start and held the vision for me.

To Dr. Patricia Fitzgerald, whose healing mastery helped me unplug and recharge.

To Bertrand and Roberta Babinet, who helped me stay healthy and balanced.

To Drs. Ron and Mary Hulnick, who have been my mentors in unconditional loving and who, through the

University of Santa Monica, have ushered so many—including me—to find their hearts' calling.

To Priyanka Boghani, for her meticulous line edits.

To Laura Koch and Sally Mason of Hay House, who in their beautiful calm way keep things going to completion.

To Christy Salinas, director of creative and print production at Hay House, who, together with the talented designer Julie Davison, is responsible for the perfect cover for the message of the book.

To Paul Kaye, whose unbound heart propelled my own unbinding.

Most of all, to my beloved sister, Arianna, whose steady love and support are the wind beneath my wings.

And to my wondrous nieces, Christina and Isabella, to whom the book is dedicated, with my wish that their hearts will always be full.

Join Us!

Visit www.unbindingtheheart.com

Download the free guided meditation

Share your story

ABOUT THE AUTHOR

Agapi Stassinopoulos was born and raised in Athens, Greece. At age 18, she entered the prestigious Royal Academy of Dramatic Art in London and afterward became a member of the Young Vic. She moved to the United States to do film and television, and later attended the University of Santa Monica, where she completed her Master's in Psychology.

While her sister, Arianna Huffington, was doing research for her book about Greek mythology, Agapi's love for the gods and goddesses was ignited and led to two books of her own—*Conversations with the Goddesses* and *Gods and Goddesses in Love*—as well as a one-woman show and a PBS special. She also co-produced and co-hosted a documentary called "Quest for the Gods," shot on location in Greece.

Agapi has been invited to speak at various international events and global conferences, and has also spoken about health and well-being for The Spirit of Women organization, which represents hundreds of hospitals around the country.

An inspiring speaker, Agapi conducts seminars worldwide for both men and women, empowering them to recognize their individual gifts and create the lives they want. She is a frequent blogger for *The Huffington Post*.

Website: **www.unbindingtheheart.com**

We hope you enjoyed this Hay House book. If you'd like to receive our online catalog featuring additional information on Hay House books and products, or if you'd like to find out more about the Hay Foundation, please contact:

Hay House, Inc., P.O. Box 5100, Carlsbad, CA 92018-5100
(760) 431-7695 or (800) 654-5126
(760) 431-6948 (fax) or (800) 650-5115 (fax)
www.hayhouse.com® • **www.hayfoundation.org**

Published and distributed in Australia by: Hay House Australia Pty. Ltd., 18/36 Ralph St., Alexandria NSW 2015 • *Phone:* 612-9669-4299 *Fax:* 612-9669-4144 • www.hayhouse.com.au

Published and distributed in the United Kingdom by: Hay House UK, Ltd., 292B Kensal Rd., London W10 5BE • *Phone:* 44-20-8962-1230 • *Fax:* 44-20-8962-1239 • www.hayhouse.co.uk

Published and distributed in the Republic of South Africa by: Hay House SA (Pty), Ltd., P.O. Box 990, Witkoppen 2068 *Phone/Fax:* 27-11-467-8904 • www.hayhouse.co.za

Published in India by: Hay House Publishers India, Muskaan Complex, Plot No. 3, B-2, Vasant Kunj, New Delhi 110 070 *Phone:* 91-11-4176-1620 • *Fax:* 91-11-4176-1630 www.hayhouse.co.in

Distributed in Canada by: Raincoast, 9050 Shaughnessy St., Vancouver, B.C. V6P 6E5 • *Phone:* (604) 323-7100 *Fax:* (604) 323-2600 • www.raincoast.com

---

Take Your Soul on a Vacation

Visit **www.HealYourLife.com®** to regroup, recharge, and reconnect with your own magnificence. Featuring blogs, mind-body-spirit news, and life-changing wisdom from Louise Hay and friends.

Visit **www.HealYourLife.com** today!